i

Uganda:

Malaria Operational Plan FY 2014

Table of Contents

Abbreviations and Acronyms

ACT	Artemisinin-based combination therapy
AL	Artemether-lumefantrine
AMFm	Affordable Medicines Facility - malaria
ANC	Antenatal care
BCC	Behavior change communication
CDC	Centers for Disease Control and Prevention
DFID	UK Department for International Development
DHS	Demographic and Health Survey
DOT	Directly observed treatment
EPI	Expanded Program on Immunization
FANC	Focused antenatal care
FY	Fiscal year
GHI	Global Health Initiative
Global Fund	Global Fund to Fight AIDS, Tuberculosis, and Malaria
GOU	Government of Uganda
HBMF	Home-based management of fever
HMIS	Health management information system
HRH	Human Resources for Health
iCCM	Integrated Community Case Management
IPTp	Intermittent preventive treatment in pregnancy
IRS	Indoor residual spraying
ITN	Insecticide-treated net
LLIN	Long-lasting insecticide-treated net
MIS	Malaria Indicator Survey
M&E	Monitoring and evaluation
MOH	Ministry of Health
NDA	National Drug Authority
NMCP	National Malaria Control Program
NMS	National Medical Stores
PEPFAR	President's Emergency Plan for HIV/AIDS Relief
PMI	President's Malaria Initiative
PNFP	Private not for profit health facilities
QA/QC	Quality assurance/Quality control
RBM	Roll Back Malaria
RDT	Rapid diagnostic test
SP	Sulfadoxine-pyrimethamine
USAID	United States Agency for International Development
USG	United States Government
WHO	World Health Organization

I. EXECUTIVE SUMMARY

Malaria prevention and control is a major foreign assistance objective of the U.S. Government (USG). In May 2009, President Barack Obama announced the Global Health Initiative (GHI), a comprehensive effort to reduce the burden of disease and promote healthy communities and families around the world. Through the GHI, the United States will help partner countries improve health outcomes, with a particular focus on improving the health of women, newborns and children.

The President's Malaria Initiative (PMI) is a core component of the GHI, along with HIV/AIDS, tuberculosis, maternal and child health, and nutrition. PMI was launched in June 2005 as a 5-year, $1.2 billion initiative to rapidly scale up malaria prevention and treatment interventions and reduce malaria-related mortality by 50% in 15 high-burden countries in sub-Saharan Africa. With passage of the Lantos-Hyde Act, the PMI goal was adjusted to halve the burden of malaria in 70 percent of the at-risk populations of sub-Saharan Africa, thereby removing malaria as a major public health problem and one of the two objectives for sub-Saharan Africa is to reduce malaria-related mortality by 70% in the original 15 countries by the end of 2015, of which Uganda is one.

Malaria is Uganda's leading cause of morbidity and mortality. According to the Ministry of Health (MOH), malaria accounts for 25-40% of outpatient visits to health facilities and is responsible for nearly half of inpatient pediatric deaths. Results of the 2011 Demographic and Health Survey (DHS) show an improvement over the 2009 Malaria Indicator Survey (MIS) with 60% of households nationwide owning at least one insecticide-treated net (ITN); 47% of pregnant women and 43% of children under five having slept under an ITN the night before the survey. In addition, the DHS shows that 43% of children under five had been treated with an antimalarial drug on the same day or the next day after the onset of fever, while the proportion receiving an artemisinin-based combination therapy (ACT) was 30%. However, the UDHS report shows a decline in women receiving intermittent preventive treatment during pregnancy (IPTp) from 32% to 25%.

Alongside the efforts of the Government of Uganda, PMI, the Global Fund and the United Kingdom's Department for International Development (DFID) are the three main contributors to malaria control in Uganda, with additional support from a range of other donors. Uganda has three active grants from the Global Fund: Round 7 Phase 2 which will provide an additional 15.5 million ITNs to achieve universal coverage; Round 10 Phase 1 and 2 will cover approximately 45 million ACT treatments, 6.7 million ITNs and 45 million rapid diagnostic tests (RDTs) through 2016. In calendar year 2013, DFID in collaboration with PMI Uganda, will provide 5 million ITNs to contribute to the universal coverage campaign planned for later in the year. World Vision is providing additional 500,000 ITNs.

PMI/Uganda's fiscal year (FY) 2014 Malaria Operational Plan was developed in close collaboration with the National Malaria Control Program (NMCP) and other major partners during a team planning visit carried out in April 2013. The proposed activities fit in well with the draft Uganda 2010/11-2014/15 National Malaria Control Strategy and complement the contributions of other donors. The proposed FY 2014 PMI budget for Uganda is $33 million.

The planned activities with FY 2014 funding are:

Indoor Residual Spraying (IRS): The ten northern districts of Kitgum, Lamwo, Pader, Agago, Apac, Kole, Oyam, Gulu, Amuru, and Nwoya were sprayed with funding from PMI during calendar year 2013 treating over 850,000 houses and protecting approximately 3 million people. These districts have historically had the highest prevalence rates of malaria country-wide. With FY 2014 funds, PMI will continue to support IRS campaigns, but to manage insecticide resistance, PMI will switch from twice-yearly spraying with a carbamate insecticide to once a year spraying with a long-lasting organophosphate. This will afford PMI the opportunity to spray at least seven districts to reflect current malaria epidemiology at reduced labor costs while increasing support for malaria case surveillance, and entomological and vector resistance monitoring. These changes will help better inform future IRS strategy in Uganda. PMI will continue to support capacity-building of MOH staff to conduct and oversee IRS.

Insecticide-treated nets (ITNs): With FY 2012 funds, PMI procured 1,200,000 ITNs and distributed 200,000 through antenatal care (ANC) clinics in the central, eastern, and western regions and about 650,000 via mass campaigns in four districts in the eastern region of the country. With FY 2014 funds, PMI will procure and distribute 1 million free ITNs through ANC clinics to sustain high net ownership following the universal coverage campaign supported by the Global Fund, PMI/DFID and World Vision. To ensure proper net usage, PMI will use mass media and community mobilization strategies to increase knowledge and promote proper and consistent use of ITNs. This effort, combined with ITNs programmed from Global Fund Round 7 Phase 2, is expected to increase national household ownership of one or more ITNs from 60% to 85%.

Intermittent preventive treatment of pregnant women (IPTp): In the last year, PMI supported the training and on-the-job supervision of 5,651 health workers in integrated management of malaria including malaria in pregnancy, strengthening of private health sector capacity to implement malaria in pregnancy interventions according to national guidelines, and monitoring of Sulfadoxine-Pyrimethamine (SP) stock levels in health facilities to help maintain adequate SP supplies for IPTp. With FY 2014 funds, PMI will continue to provide on-site training and supportive supervision related to malaria in pregnancy to ANC workers in the public and private sector. PMI will leverage ongoing President's Emergency Plan for AIDS Relief (PEPFAR) Uganda efforts to rapidly scale up prevention from mother to child transmission of HIV as one of the strategies to enhance IPTp uptake. PMI will continue to provide safe water and drinking cups for direct observation of treatment with SP for IPTp.

Case management: In the past year, PMI worked to improve diagnostic capacity for malaria and effective case management of febrile illness in 49 districts through training of health care workers in malaria diagnosis and treatment in both the public and private sectors. In addition, ongoing technical assistance was provided for developing a strategy for a national quality assurance system for diagnostics. With FY 2014 funds, PMI will increase support for the

4

improvement of case management, in both the public and private sectors, through training, supervision, and commodities procurement. To highlight an important change in case management, PMI along with partners, will assist the NMCP in introducing intravenous artesunate as the first-line treatment for complicated malaria. At the community level, PMI will also reinstitute support for integrated community case management in select pilot districts. Additionally, FY 2014 funds will continue supporting the roll-out and use of RDTs as well as quality assurance and supportive supervision for microscopists trained with PMI support. Together with other USAID health programs and PEPFAR, PMI will strengthen the national pharmaceutical management system by improving performance and financial management, clarifying pharmaceutical policy, and establishing a transparent logistics management information system.

Monitoring and Evaluation (M&E): PMI has supported the collection of high quality malaria surveillance data from selected health facilities since 2006. Surveillance data are used by the NMCP and other malaria stakeholders to monitor trends in malaria burden and for programmatic decision making. PMI also continued to provide support to the NMCP for surveillance and M&E capacity building, including data use workshops at national and local levels. The results of the 2011 DHS highlighted the gains in key malaria intervention coverage, including ownership of at least one ITN per household from 16% to 60% (2006 & 2011 DHS). With FY 2014 funds, PMI will leverage the new USG integrated health regional platform approach for health systems strengthening and focus on improving the quality of malaria data and their use by the NMCP. As a part of this process, PMI will continue to support the national, regional, district and health facility-level health management information system (HMIS) activities including training health workers on the new HMIS tools and supportive supervision. PMI will continue to build capacity in the NMCP M&E unit by providing support for data management tools and training. The current malaria surveillance sites will continue their role as malaria reference centers and provide outreach to health facilities in the nearby districts through training, supervision support, and quality assurance and control for case management - with a strong focus on diagnostics - and data management. The lessons learned from sentinel surveillance scale up will be used to improve case management and data quality in the surrounding health facilities while taking into account limited resources. Improved data quality and use will assist PMI and the NMCP to evaluate the effect of interventions and better direct future strategic decisions around activities such as IRS. In addition, PMI will help support the 2014 MIS.

Health Systems Strengthening and Integration: With support from PMI, PEPFAR and USAID health funds, Human Resources for Health (HRH) strengthening activities, a wage bill was introduced and passed by the Uganda parliament 2012, and there was increased recruitment of additional staff in key cadres, especially at the health center level four (HC-4) level increasing the rate of retention of critical staff from 53% in 2011 to 70% in 2012. With FY 2014 funds, PMI in collaboration with USAID health programs and PEPFAR will continue to work through USAID/Uganda's regionally-focused and district-based integrated service delivery programming to: a) train staff and to improve service quality through supportive supervision, b) strengthen the national pharmaceutical supply chain system through technical assistance, and c) provide technical assistance to support staff performance evaluation, financial management, revision of pharmaceutical policy, and to establish a transparent, well-performing logistics management information system.

Crosscutting behavior change communication (BCC): With FY 2012 funds, PMI activities reached 4 million Ugandans with key malaria messages on the importance of net use, prompt care seeking, and prevention of malaria during pregnancy. The communication approaches include radio talk shows with 244 community listening groups, and through village health assistants' community mobilization and school activities. With FY 2014 funds, PMI will continue to support targeted and evidence-based BCC at national, district, and community level to encourage consistent and correct use of ITNs, usage of IPTp by pregnant women, prompt care seeking for suspected malaria and parasitological-based diagnosis, and appropriate treatment for those with confirmed malaria.

II. STRATEGY

INTRODUCTION

GLOBAL HEALTH INITIATIVE

Malaria prevention and control is a major foreign assistance objective of the U.S. Government (USG). In May 2009, President Barack Obama announced the Global Health Initiative (GHI) to promote healthy communities and families around the world. Through the GHI, the United States will help partner countries improve health outcomes, with a particular focus on improving the health of women, newborns, and children. The GHI is a global commitment to invest in healthy and productive lives, building upon and expanding the USG's successes in addressing specific diseases and issues.

The GHI aims to maximize the impact the United States achieves for every health dollar it invests in a sustainable way. The GHI's business model is based on: implementing a woman- and girl-centered approach; increasing impact and efficiency through strategic coordination and programmatic integration; strengthening and leveraging key partnerships, multilateral organizations, and private contributions; encouraging country ownership and investing in country-led plans and health systems; improving metrics, monitoring and evaluation; and promoting research and innovation. The GHI builds on the USG's accomplishments in global health by accelerating progress in health delivery and investing in a more lasting and shared approach through the strengthening of health systems.

THE PRESIDENT'S MALARIA INITIATIVE

The President's Malaria Initiative (PMI) is a core component of the GHI, along with HIV/AIDS, and tuberculosis. PMI was launched in June 2005 as a five-year, $1.2 billion initiative to rapidly scale up malaria prevention and treatment interventions and reduce malaria-related mortality by 50% in 15 high-burden countries in sub-Saharan Africa. With passage of the 2008 Lantos-Hyde Act, funding for PMI was extended and, as part of the GHI, the goal of PMI was adjusted to reduce malaria-related mortality by 70% in the original 15 countries by the end of 2015. This will be achieved by reaching 85% coverage of the most vulnerable groups — children under five years of age and pregnant women — with proven preventive and therapeutic measures, including artemisinin-based combination therapies (ACTs), insecticide-treated nets (ITNs), intermittent preventive treatment of pregnant women (IPTp), and indoor residual spraying (IRS). Through GHI and PMI, the USG is committed to working closely with host governments and within existing national malaria control plans. Efforts are coordinated with other national and international partners, including the Global Fund to Fight AIDS, Tuberculosis and Malaria (Global Fund), Roll Back Malaria (RBM), the World Bank Malaria Booster Program, and the non-governmental and private sectors, to ensure that investments are complementary and that RBM and Millennium Development Goals are achieved.

This FY 2014 Malaria Operational Plan (MOP) presents a detailed implementation plan for the ninth year of the President's Malaria Initiative (PMI) in Uganda, based on PMI's multi-year strategy and plan and the National Malaria Control Program's (NMCP) five-year strategy. It was developed in consultation with the Uganda NMCP and stakeholders involved with Uganda malaria prevention and control. The activities that PMI is proposing support the 2010/11-2014/15 National Malaria Control Strategy and Plan, and build on investments made by PMI and other partners to improve and expand malaria-related services. This document briefly reviews the current status of malaria control policies and interventions in Uganda, describes progress to date, identifies challenges and unmet needs, and provides a description of planned FY 2014 activities. The total amount requested for PMI in Uganda in FY 2014 is $33 million.

USAID/Uganda's Country Development Cooperation Strategy implements President Obama's new U.S. Global Development Policy. The strategy coordinates other USG activities within the context of host country and other donor activities. The Presidential initiatives currently underway in Uganda are: PMI, President's Emergency Plan for AIDS Relief (PEPFAR), Global Health Initiative (GHI), the Global Climate Change Initiative, and Feed the Future.

All Presidential initiatives and other health and education programs under USAID Uganda Development Objective 3, "improved health and nutrition status in focus areas and population groups," are linked by the common goal of transitioning Uganda to a modern and prosperous country. While each of the presidential initiatives, including PMI, have critical goals and objectives that the USAID Mission in Uganda is committed to achieving, Development Objective 3 also prioritizes the cross-cutting goals of the Mission: strategic integration of health services, strengthening health systems, supporting decentralized social sector services, engaging the private sector and civil society, and increased civic engagement and advocacy at the community level. Implemented activities aimed at reaching these goals will help the government and private sector tackle the heavy disease burden, malnutrition, and unmet need for family planning by improving health service delivery systems. These USAID Mission priorities carried out by objective 3 seek to ensure a contextually appropriate approach to health and development in Uganda. Collective and collaborative engagement of five presidential initiatives under GHI framework will accelerate the achievement of specific PMI goals and objectives. A large part of the strategy will rely on strengthening the health systems that underlie service delivery with the overall aim of achieving the public health objective of morbidity and mortality reduction among the Ugandan population.

MALARIA SITUATION IN UGANDA

Malaria is highly endemic in 95% of the country with approximately 90% of the population (estimated at 32 million people) at risk. The remaining 5% of the country consists of unstable and epidemic-prone transmission areas in the highlands of the south and west, along the eastern border with Kenya, and the northeastern border with South Sudan. Malaria transmission is persistently high in some areas of northern Uganda. For example, before starting IRS, Apac

District reported an entomological inoculation rate of 1,600[1]. That is more than four infected mosquito bites every night and is among the highest recorded in the world. In most parts of the country, favorable temperature and rainfall allow intense vector propagation and perennial malaria transmission.

Figure 1: Malaria Endemicity in Uganda

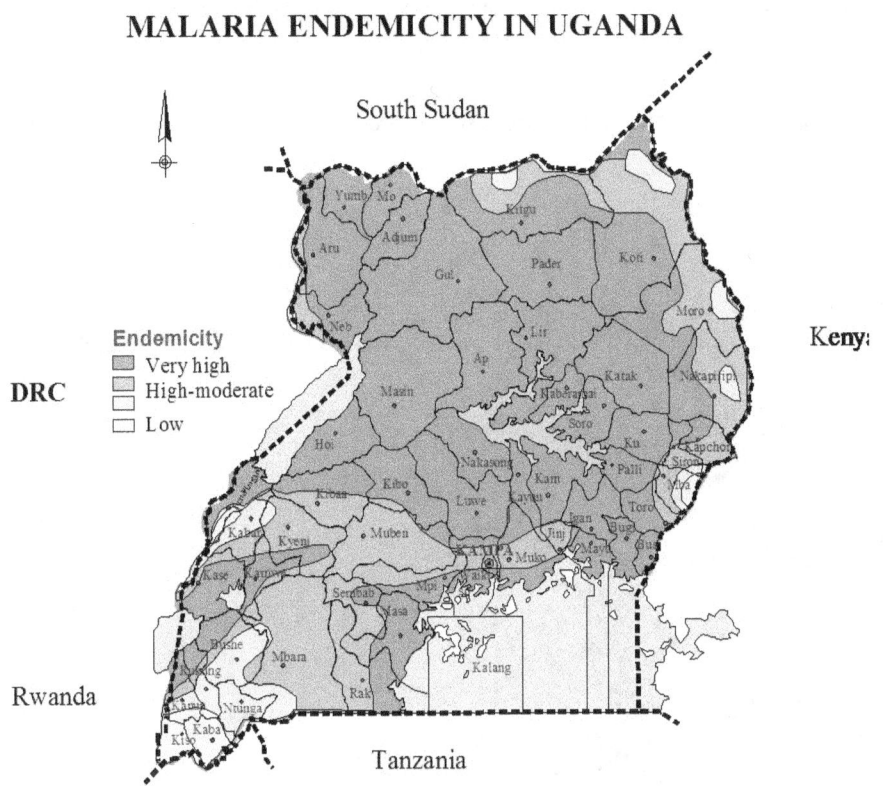

The most common malaria vectors are *Anopheles gambiae s.l.* and *An. funestus. An, gambiae* is the dominant species in most places, while *An. funestus* is generally found at higher altitudes and during the short dry seasons (September through November), when permanent water bodies are the most common breeding sites. In some areas of northern Uganda, such as Apac and Oyam, *A. funestus* is the most common vector that feeds primarily on humans and also takes blood meals from domestic animals. *An. gambiae s.l.* and *An. funestus* feed and rest indoors, making ITNs and IRS viable vector control strategies.

The Uganda Malaria Indicator Survey (MIS), conducted in late 2009, showed that *Plasmodium falciparum* is responsible for 99% of malaria cases. *P. malariae,* accounts for 0.2% of cases as a mono-infection but is more commonly found as a mixed infection with *P. falciparum* (up to 2.7% of childhood infections in highly endemic areas). Both *P. vivax* and *P. ovale* are rare and do not exceed 2% of malaria cases in Uganda.

---

[1] Okello PE, Van Bortel W, Byaruhanga AM, Correwyn A, Roelants P, Talisuna A, D'Alessandro U, Coosemans M. 2006. Variation in malaria transmission intensity in seven sites throughout Uganda.Am J Trop Med Hyg. Aug;75(2):219-25

Malaria prevalence among children 0 to 59 months of age by microscopy in the 2009 MIS showed that 42% tested positive for malaria. Prevalence was higher in rural areas than in urban areas (47% versus 15% using microscopy) and ranged from 5% in Kampala to 63% in the mid northern region. Survey data indicated that anemia is also a significant public health problem in Uganda. Six out of ten Ugandan children 0 to 59 months of age are anemic (hemoglobin concentration below 11 g/dL): 21% are mildly anemic (10.0 – 10.9 g/dL), 30% are moderately anemic (8.0 – 9.9 g/dL), and 10% are severely anemic (< 8.0 g/dL). The map below shows the percentage of children 0-59 months of age testing positive for malaria with microscopy (with anemia rates in parentheses).

Figure 2: Malaria and Anemia Prevalence (in parentheses) among Children 0-59 Months

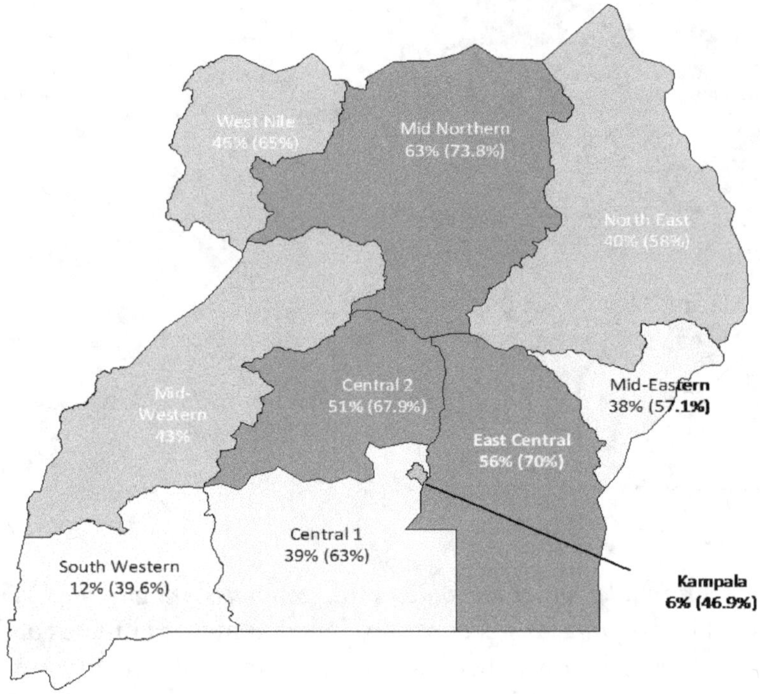

MALARIA CONTROL STRATEGY FOR UGANDA

The NMCP was established in 1995 by the Government of Uganda (GOU) to direct and guide the day-to-day implementation of the National Malaria Control Strategy. The role of the NMCP at central level is to support the implementation of the National Malaria Control Strategy through policy formulation; setting standards and quality assurance; resource mobilization; capacity development and technical support; malaria epidemic control; coordination of malaria research; and monitoring and evaluation. The NMCP has support from multiple partners including PMI.

The NMCP's strategy for malaria prevention and control employs all proven interventions: vector control through IRS, ITNs and larviciding; prevention of malaria in pregnancy through ITNs and IPTp; effective case management including parasite-based diagnosis and treatment with ACTs, and monitoring and evaluation (M&E) of all components of the program.

INTEGRATION, COLLABORATION, AND COORDINATION

- The NMCP has benefited from increasing support from various partners. These include: The Global Fund to Fight AIDS, Tuberculosis and Malaria (Global Fund), which currently focuses its resources for Uganda on the procurement of malaria commodities, including the support for procurement of 15.5 million long-lasting insecticide-treated nets (LLINs) and ACTs and RDTs for diagnosis and treatment malaria. The Round 10 application for $156 million, will provide a five-year supply of ACTs to the public and private not-for-profit sector, including integrated community case management (a program that includes home based management of fever (HBMF)); procurement of microscopes and scale-up of rapid diagnostic tests (RDTs); routine distribution of ITNs through antenatal care (ANC) and Expanded Program on Immunization (EPI) clinics; behavior change communication (BCC); support for strengthening the health management information system (HMIS); drug and insecticide resistance monitoring; health facility surveys; and basic program support to the NMCP.

- The United Kingdom's Department for International Development (DFID) – made a commitment in 2010 to significantly increase support for health and malaria control specifically in Uganda. DFID funds are supporting the procurement and distribution of LLINs for the 2013/14 universal coverage and commodity surveillance program with the potential for support of additional activities in the future.

- World Health Organization (WHO)/Uganda, which provides M&E technical assistance.

- Clinton Health Access Initiative – has supported activities related to Affordable Medicines Facility – malaria (AMFm). CHAI has provided technical support to the AMFm and is currently providing technical assistance to the NMCP to develop a strategy for effective case management including diagnosis and appropriate treatment with an ACT in both the public and private sectors in Uganda.

While the NMCP and its partners follow the RBM Strategic Plan and the "three ones" principle (one coordinating mechanism, one plan, and one M&E system), there are still major weaknesses in coordination of activities, leading to potential duplication of efforts and suboptimal resource utilization. Improving this coordination is critical in light of the increasing number of partners and resources for malaria control.

Integration, collaboration, and coordination within USG

As part of the GHI, the USG has developed an expanded PMI strategy prioritizing integration of malaria prevention and treatment activities with maternal and child health, HIV/AIDS, neglected tropical diseases, and tuberculosis programs; strengthening host country health systems to ensure sustainability; and ensuring a women-centered approach for malaria prevention and treatment activities at both the community and health facility levels.

In Uganda, PMI will contribute to the goals of the GHI by:

- Supporting health systems strengthening efforts, including:

a) Strengthening supply chain management for health commodities at the central, regional, and district level (costs included under the Pharmaceutical Management section);
b) Addressing human resources for health and developing the capacity of the health workforce at national and district level (costs included under the Health Systems Strengthening and Capacity Building section);
c) Strengthening the quality and timely use of HMIS data (costs included under the M&E section);

- Supporting integration of malaria control in maternal and child health and prevention of mother to child transmission of HIV programs to promote a harmonized approach for district-based health delivery (costs included under the Case Management section);
  a) Improving the quality and use of ANC through integrated support for focused antenatal care (FANC) (costs included under the IPTp section);
  b) Working with PEPFAR to improve laboratory diagnostic capacity through the development of Quality Assurance/Quality Control (QA/QC) systems along with training and supervision (costs included under the Diagnostics section);
  c) Continued support with HIV/AIDS and tuberculosis programs for public-private partnerships (cost sharing with private companies) and capacity building (costs included under the IPTp and Case Management section);
  d) Continued support for integrated supportive supervision of health workers at central and district level (costs included under the Case Management section).

PMI GOALS, TARGETS, AND INDICATORS

The goal of PMI is to reduce malaria-associated mortality by 70% compared to pre-Initiative levels in the 15 original PMI countries. By the end of 2014, PMI will assist Uganda to achieve the following targets in populations at risk for malaria:
- >90% of households with a pregnant woman and/or children under five will own at least one ITN;
- 85% of children under five will have slept under an ITN the previous night;
- 85% of pregnant women will have slept under an ITN the previous night;
- 85% of houses in geographic areas targeted for IRS will have been sprayed;
- 85% of pregnant women and children under five will have slept under an ITN the previous night or in a house that has been protected by IRS;
- 85% of women who have completed a pregnancy in the last two years will have received two or more doses of IPTp during that pregnancy;
- 85% of government health facilities have ACTs available for treatment of uncomplicated malaria, and:
- 85% of children under five with suspected or confirmed malaria will have received treatment with ACTs within 24 hours of onset of their symptoms.

PROGRESS ON INDICATORS TO DATE

The table below shows coverage and impact data from the 2011 Uganda Demographic and Health Survey (DHS) and the 2009 MIS:

Indicator	Baseline (2006 DHS)	MIS (2009)	DHS (2011)
Percentage of households that own at least one ITN	16%	47%	60%
Proportion of children under five years of age sleeping under an ITN the previous night	10%	33%	43%
Proportion of pregnant women sleeping under an ITN the previous night	10%	44%	47%
Proportion of pregnant women who received at least two doses of IPTp during antenatal care	16%	32%	25%
Prevalence of parasitemia (by microscopy) in children 0 – 59 months	N/A	42%	N/A
Prevalence of anemia in children 0 – 59 months (Hg < 10.9g/dl)[2]&[3]	N/A	62%	50%[2]
Prevalence of severe anemia in children 0 – 59 months (Hg < 8 g/dl)	N/A	10%	3%

OTHER RELEVANT EVIDENCE OF PROGRESS

In 2010/11, two small scale community-based surveys were conducted with support from PMI. The first was to assess the incremental effect of IRS using carbamates on prevalence of anemia and parasitemia; it compared data from two districts that receive IRS, Apac and Pader, to one that has not received IRS, Lira, in northern Uganda, with all districts receiving similar support for ITNs and case management for malaria. The second survey was conducted in the central region of the country in late 2010 evaluating the coverage and usage of ITNs after the targeted mass distribution campaign that occurred in early 2010.

The anemia and parasitemia study in the north showed that among children under five years of age, prevalence of anemia (Hb <11.0 g/dL) was 39% in Apac (IRS), 37% in Pader (IRS), versus 53% in Lira districts (no IRS). Similar differences were found in parasite prevalence with 37% in

---

[2] Roll Back Malaria, MEASURE Evaluation, USAID, UNICEF, World Health Organization, MACEPA, CDC. Guidelines for Core Population-Based Indicators. MEASURE Evaluation: Calverton, MD.

[3] Prevalence of anemia, based on hemoglobin levels, is adjusted for altitude using CDC formulas (CDC, 1998). Women and children with <7.0g/dl of hemoglobin have severe anemia, women and children with 7.0 – 9.9g/dl have moderate anemia, and non-pregnant women with 10.0- 11.9g/dl and children and pregnant women with 10.0 – 10.9g/dl have mild anemia

Apac, 17% in Pader, versus 50% in Lira[4]. The central region ITN survey showed an increase in households that owned at least one ITN from 24% (2009 MIS) to 63% and usage among children under five years of age from 11% to 43%. These increases were confirmed in the 2011DHS results with 60% of all households (national level) with at least one ITN and 43% of children under five years of age sleeping under an ITN the night prior to the survey in households with an ITN.

Data from sentinel surveillance in Apac District in the north, where some of the highest rates of malaria transmission have been recorded, show that IRS in combination with support for case management and ITNs have contributed to lower rates of slide positivity among those presenting to the sentinel site health facility. See figure below.

Figure 3: Slide Positivity Rates and IRS Campaigns in Apac District, 2009—2013

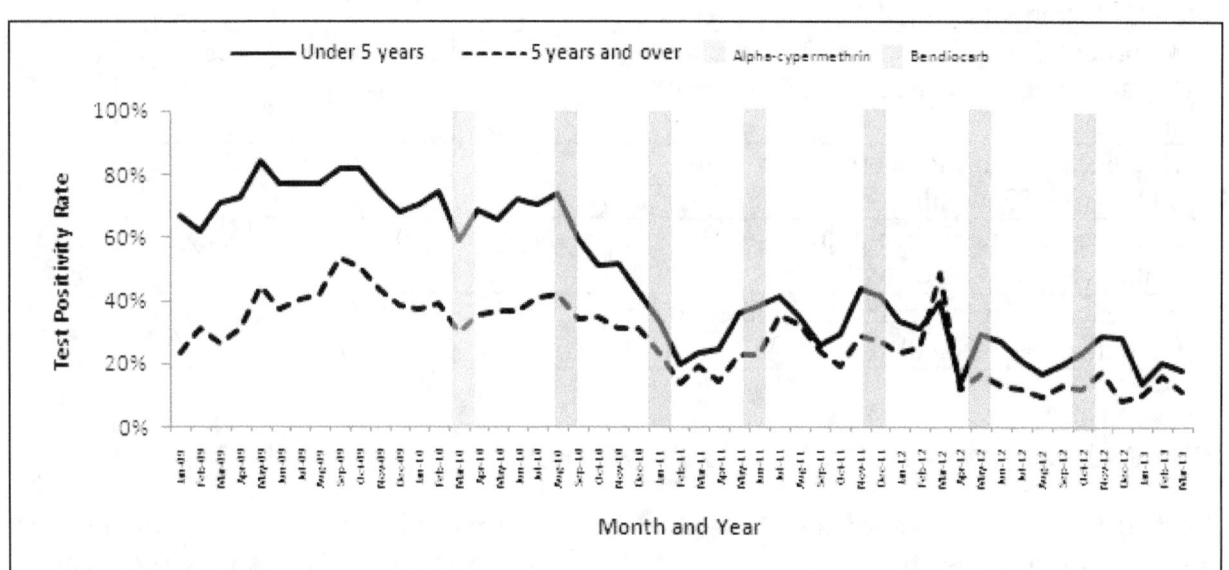

As one of the RBM partners, Malaria Consortium with funds from DFID's Program Partnership Agreement (PPA) is conducting a series of studies:

(1) The Pyrethroid Resistance Management Study is a retrospective cohort study on pyrethroid resistance in three different pyrethroid use zones across nine districts in Uganda. The aim of the study is to support the NMCP to gain an in-depth understanding of the threat posed by insecticide resistance, its impact, and factors that contribute to its spread as well as its management. This information will be used to support the NMCP to develop practical approaches to counter the problem in order to prolong the useful life of effective vector control interventions such as IRS and LLINs. Data analysis for this study is underway and results are expected in July 2013.

(2) The Beyond Garki project is monitoring changes in malaria epidemiology in relation to available interventions in western and northern Uganda. The purpose of this study is to support

[4] Steinhardt LC, Adoke Y, Nasr S, Wiegand RE, Rubahika D, Serwanga A, Wanzira H, Lavoy G, Kamya M, Dorsey G, Filler S: The effect of indoor residual spraying on malaria and anaemia in a high transmission area of Northern Uganda. Am Trop Med Hyg 2013, 88:855-861 doi:10.4269/ajtmh.12-0747.

the Ministry of Health (MOH) and the District Health Management Teams in Kyankwanzi and Apac to monitor the changing malaria epidemiology within the context of multiple interventions and assess the conditions necessary to reduce transmission below the critical level. This study is an analytical cross-sectional survey, conducted repeatedly through continuous, longitudinal collection of climatic data, morbidity data at health facilities, household, malariometric and serological data, therapeutic efficacy studies, and entomological data. Round 1 survey data collection, data entry and cleaning are completed. Data analysis is underway and results are expected in July 2013. Round 2 survey data collection is ongoing including drug efficacy studies and climate monitoring.

(3) In collaboration with Foundation for Innovative New Diagnostics and with support from Malaria Consortium's Pioneer Project, Malaria Consortium is evaluating the use, utility and acceptability of positive control wells for malaria RDTs in routine health care settings and at community level (with village health teams) in two malaria-endemic districts (Kiboga and Kyankwanzi), in order to guide rational implementation strategies for positive control wells. Results of this trial are expected in early 2014.

(4) In light of the low uptake of two doses of IPTp (IPTp2) observed nationally, Malaria Consortium is conducting a study to assess barriers to uptake of two courses of IPTp. The project aims to (1) determine which barriers may still pose challenges to IPTp uptake in Uganda, and identify new barriers, with a focus on: barriers to receiving a first dose of SP as part of focused antenatal care (FANC) and barriers to receiving a second dose of SP as part of FANC for women who have already received one dose, (2) develop a set of recommendations, including a potential intervention, which will improve uptake of IPTp2 and enable the Uganda NMCP to meet the goal of 85% coverage of IPTp2. This study is in very early stages and the results are expected to be available in 2014.

In spite of efforts to address challenges in uptake through assurance of adequate stocks at health facilities, training and support supervision of health workers, provision of commodities (cups and safe drinking water) for directly observed therapy, and BCC, IPTp uptake has remained low nationally. The national estimate from the 2011 DHS shows that this has dropped to 25% (from 32% in the 2009 MIS). However, in PMI focus areas percentage of mothers of children 0-11 months who received two or more doses of IPTp during their last pregnancy is as high as 66% (Stop Malaria Project – lot quality assurance data 2012).

PMI SUPPORT STRATEGY

PMI's strategy for Uganda has been to support the NMCP's strategic goals and priorities. As these are diverse, PMI has prioritized the key intervention areas and supports capacity building at all levels of the health system. PMI has focused on provision of comprehensive malaria services in 49 high-burden districts and covering gaps that remain after the Global Fund and other donor support have been considered. These high-burden districts are also often priority districts under the USAID Uganda Country Development Cooperation Strategy so that PMI investments are also leveraging other health and development program investments in priority Mission integrated regional project(s).

In FY 2014 PMI will leverage the USG's regional integration strategy in Uganda to strengthen and improve service delivery through continuing to build capacity of NMCP while:

- Strengthening regional/district level technical capacity
- Ensuring that correct and consistent use of net and net culture improved after the 2013 universal net campaign
- Improving malaria disease surveillance to provide evidence for malaria control strategy
- Focusing on USG program implementation monitoring to ensure investments are delivering expected results
- Refocusing IRS strategy to reflect the current risk of malaria, targeting higher transmission areas.

III. OPERATIONAL PLAN

INDOOR RESIDUAL SPRAYING

Background

IRS is a proven intervention and it is prioritized by the NMCP when feasible, especially in high transmission settings and high-risk situations (e.g., internally displaced people's camps). Prior to PMI, the NMCP had not conducted any large-scale spray campaigns since the 1960s. In 2006, PMI supported a large-scale IRS program in the epidemic-prone southwestern highland district of Kabale and achieved impressive results both in terms of coverage and impact. In 2007, PMI targeted its support to high-risk sub-counties of Kabale and extended support to the neighboring district of Kanungu and four northern districts (Kitgum, Pader, Gulu, and Amuru), protecting large populations of internally displaced persons. After consultation with the NMCP, PMI then scaled-back support of IRS in Kabale and Kanungu and prioritized resources to the highest transmission areas of northern Uganda (Kitgum, Pader, Apac, and Oyam), areas with the highest concentration of camps and some of the highest rates of malaria transmission in the world. In 2005, a study estimated that on average, each person in this region received 1,600 malaria-infected bites every year,[5] and the population prevalence of malaria parasitemia among children under five in 2010 was 56%.[6]

Since 2009, PMI has concentrated its support for IRS in ten northern districts: Kitgum, Agago, Lamwo, Pader, Amuru, Nwoya, Gulu, Oyam, Kole, and Apac. IRS was initially conducted with pyrethroids in all districts except Apac and Oyam, which were sprayed with DDT in 2008. Due to insecticide resistance to both insecticides, a change to carbamates was made in 2010. Targeted household coverage has been consistently high (above 90%).

IRS is conducted prior to the transmission peaks, where it is expected to have the greatest impact on malaria transmission; insecticide selection is based on vector susceptibility studies. Routine entomological monitoring has shown that the vector densities of sprayed households have fallen

---

[5] Okello P. *et al* (2006), Variation in malaria transmission intensity in seven sites throughout Uganda. *Am. J. Trop. Med. Hyg.,75(2):219–225.*
[6] Proietti C *et al* (2011), Continuing intense malaria transmission in northern Uganda. *American Journal of Tropical Medicine and Hygiene ; 84(5): 830-7.*

significantly since beginning IRS.[7] Malaria data at PMI-supported sentinel sites and other government facilities are also showing downward trends of malaria cases. The 2011 anemia and parasitemia survey comparing districts that received IRS to a district without IRS showed significant reductions in both parasitemia and anemia in the IRS districts.[8, 10]

Engagement in spraying operations of vector control officers, health assistants, district local government personnel, and NMCP personnel at central and district levels has increased steadily since 2006. As a result of this increased capacity, in 2012 the MOH carried out a round of IRS in Kumi district using GOU funds. In addition, the NMCP continues to participate in planning, implementation and monitoring of IRS activities and pursue a scale up of the IRS program in Uganda, as evidenced by GOU contribution of approximately three billion Uganda Shillings (approximately $1.2 million) to IRS in 2012 and plans to contribute a similar amount in 2013. Additional resources from the GOU, as well as other partners, will be needed to scale up IRS to additional districts.

Implementation of IRS in Uganda continues to face many challenges. Malaria transmission is intense and perennial in nearly every region of Uganda. Interrupting transmission when the transmission season lasts for ten months of the year requires multiple rounds of spraying per year or the use of insecticides with a long residual action. In 2008, PMI piloted use of DDT in Apac and Oyam Districts; however, its use was subsequently banned by a court injunction launched by organic farmers. Though the court injunction was lifted, insecticide resistance monitoring studies revealed high levels of vector resistance to DDT. Currently, the NMCP does not have a clear strategy for implementing vector control interventions. However, the GOU has indicated plans to make funding available to support some IRS and larviciding. A strategy is needed to provide clear guidelines on how the activities funded by GOU augment PMI-supported IRS and routine distribution of LLINs through ANC facilities, as well as the mass distribution of LLINs with Global Fund resources and how these interventions will be monitored and outcomes evaluated. With the exception of mass distribution of LLINs through the Global Fund Round 7, these three vector control interventions do not cover the whole country. A clear evidence-based strategy will guide and rationalize the decision-making process and implementation of different vector control interventions.

PMI supported the NMCP to update the national malaria risk map using all available or generated data (epidemiological, entomological, demographic, socioeconomic, and environmental including some remotely sensed data). The new map which was completed in 2012 reflects the current malaria interventions, economic development and changes in the environment. The development of a comprehensive vector control strategy will also allow for a more detailed analysis at the micro level (sub-district or village level) in northern Uganda that will help the NMCP and districts to develop a transition plan on how best to deploy IRS and

---

[7] Ranjith De Alwis, et al. 2011-PMI unpublished data

[8] Steinhardt L, et al. Malaria Intervention Coverage and Associated Morbidity Indicator Survey in Children under five years in Uganda. (2011) – unpublished data.

[10] Steinhardt LC, Adoke Y, Nasr S, Wiegand RE, Rubahika D, Serwanga A, Wanzira H,Lavoy G, Kamya M, Dorsey G, Filler S: The effect of indoor residual spraying on malaria and anaemia in a high transmission area of Northern Uganda. Am Trop Med Hyg 2013, 88:855-861 doi:10.4269/ajtmh.12-0747.

LLINs. The decision will also be guided by the results of PMI-supported LLIN/IRS operational research study in northern Tanzania once those results are available.

Progress during the last 12 months

To date all ten districts targeted for IRS in northern Uganda have been sprayed twice a year and a total of seven cycles of spraying for Kitgum, Pader, Agago, Apac, Oyam, Lamwo and Kole and six cycles for Amuru, Nwoya and Gulu districts have been completed. A pyrethroid insecticide was used until May 2010 and then changed to a carbamate insecticide from round three in all the districts. The project successfully conducted two rounds of spraying each year in all the target districts (now ten districts due to district subdivision) during the last 12 months, achieving a coverage rate of over 90% of the 850,000 targeted households and protecting approximately 3 million people in each spray round. IRS has proven to be successful, as evidenced by persistently low vector populations since 2010, as well as drastic reductions in malaria cases in health facilities.

Over the past year, approximately 5,000 personnel (team leaders, vector control officers/health assistants, spray operators, clinicians, and environmental officers) have been trained in various aspects of IRS operations. Currently, these individuals are actively engaged in conducting training, support supervision and monitoring activities including data collection for IRS activities. The MOH/Vector Control Division conducts all entomological activities with the PMI IRS implementing partner providing only oversight for the program.

Large-scale comprehensive community sensitization and education drives are conducted before, during, and after each spray round. These include district leader sensitizations, sub-county leader awareness programs, parish level community meetings, radio announcements, radio spots and radio talk shows.

PMI invests in building Uganda's capacity to provide supervision and oversight of IRS activities, including technical quality, entomological and environmental monitoring, and accountability. Current IRS operations are managed by a PMI implementing partner with significant support from the NMCP, National Environmental Management Authority (NEMA), and district governments. Focused, integrated training on IRS planning, management and monitoring are also provided to district health officers, environmental officers, vector control officers, and NMCP staff. PMI is supporting the development of entomological monitoring capacity and provides insectary support to ensure strong entomological monitoring capacity within the MOH.

Building of the PMI-funded insectary at Gulu University was completed in 2012. The insectary became functional in the fall of 2012 and has been in operation since. A susceptible strain of *An. gambiae* (Kisumu) was obtained from Kenya and is used extensively by the IRS implementing partner in their surveillance and monitoring efforts for the IRS program in northern Uganda. Susceptible mosquitoes are reared for use in longevity monitoring of IRS-treated households, for compliance checks on sprayed households, and are available for efficacy testing of LLINs. Additionally, the insectary is used to rear field-caught mosquito larvae for adult identification, as a training space for mosquito identification, and for testing field-caught mosquitoes for insecticide susceptibility testing by the implementing partner and university collaborators. CDC bottle bioassay training and WHO tube assay testing for resistance has been performed in the insectary over the past year.

PMI supports comprehensive vector resistance monitoring in the six different eco-epidemiological zones of Uganda biennially. The first survey conducted in 2009 uncovered a range of susceptibilities of *An. gambiae* to pyrethroid insecticides, from complete susceptibility in Apac and Wakiso Districts to full resistance to many pyrethroids in most districts. Resistance to DDT was found around the country. *Anopheles gambiae* was found to be susceptible to organophosphate (OP) and carbamate insecticides at all six sites during this survey.

The second survey occurred in October and November 2011. In all sites, *Anopheles gambiae* was susceptible to the carbamate and organophosphate insecticides tested but resistant to DDT. *Anopheles gambiae* was found to be largely resistant or tolerant to pyrethoid insecticides (23%-69% susceptibility in Apac District; 65%--92% in Kitgum District) around Uganda with the exception of full susceptibility to alpha-cypermethrin in Wakiso District. The development and spread of vector resistance to insecticides has increased the cost of IRS as replacement of pyrethroids with carbamates is more expensive and carbamates have a shorter residual life, requiring two spray cycles per year as opposed to one spray cycle for pyrethroids[11]. A change to the carbamate bendiocarb was initiated in all IRS districts in 2010. Routine wall bioassays measuring the quality and longevity of spraying in three entomological sentinel sites have been conducted and results indicate high quality spraying and that carbamate insecticides remain effective for at least 4-5 months. Emerging tolerance to bendiocarb and propoxur, both carbamate insecticides, was seen in two resistance monitoring sites in 2011 (81%--90% susceptibility in Tororo District; 96%-97% in Kanungu District)[9]. A new comprehensive vector resistance monitoring effort in the six different eco-epidemiological zones of Uganda is due to begin in September 2013 to determine the susceptibility status of malaria vectors to the four classes of WHO-approved insecticides and to monitor for changes in susceptibility of vector species to these insecticides from the last survey.

---

[9] Ibid #9

Map of mortality of Anopheles gambiae s.l. after exposure to Pyrethroids, Organophosphates, carbamate and Organochlorine in six sites in Uganda, October to November 2011

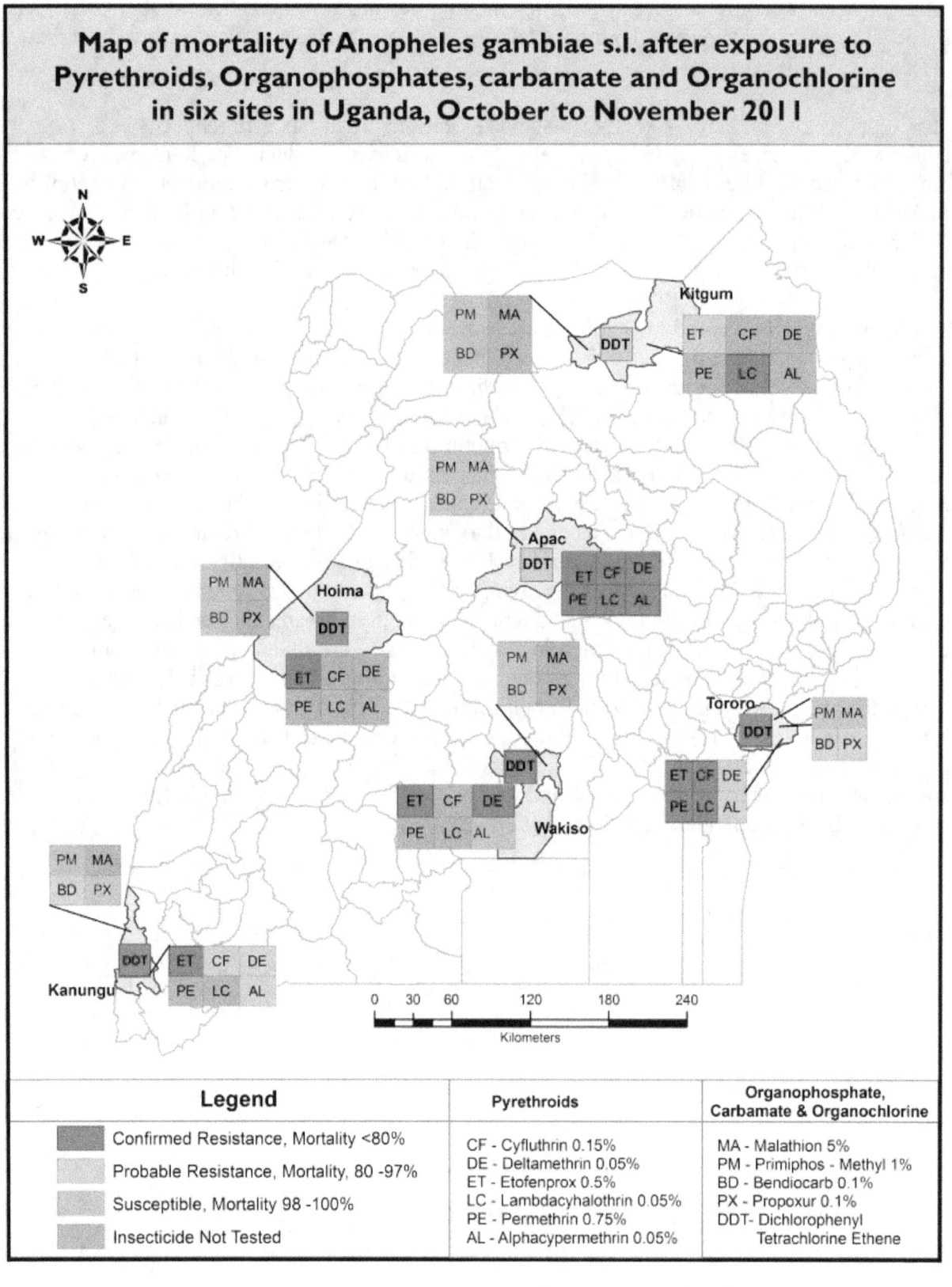

Legend	Pyrethroids	Organophosphate, Carbamate & Organochlorine
▨ Confirmed Resistance, Mortality <80%	CF - Cyfluthrin 0.15%	MA - Malathion 5%
▨ Probable Resistance, Mortality, 80 -97%	DE - Deltamethrin 0.05%	PM - Primiphos - Methyl 1%
▨ Susceptible, Mortality 98 -100%	ET - Etofenprox 0.5%	BD - Bendiocarb 0.1%
▨ Insecticide Not Tested	LC - Lambdacyhalothrin 0.05%	PX - Propoxur 0.1%
	PE - Permethrin 0.75%	DDT- Dichlorophenyl
	AL - Alphacypermethrin 0.05%	Tetrachlorine Ethene

Support for IRS continues to make up a large portion of the PMI annual budget for Uganda. Over the past few years the team has been looking for ways to reduce the operational costs of IRS and has realized some cost savings through efforts such as bicycle use by spray operators in place of trucks and increased use of district staff for planning and support supervision. In 2009, the estimated cost to spray a household was $8.40 per unit sprayed in Uganda as compared to $10 – 40 in other countries (as per a costing study by RTI). For the time period September 2009—May 2011, the cost per household was $5.84—$7.30, and per person was $1.81—$2.26.

Based on emerging carbamate tolerance in *An. gambiae,* Uganda will change to a long-lasting organophosphate (OP) insecticide in 2014. Although OP is more expensive than carbamate insecticides, needing only one spray round versus two per year will reduce labor costs to the point where total cost are likely to be slightly less for OP.

With nationwide universal coverage with ITNs planned to be achieved in early 2014, PMI will consider transitioning into two other high-burden districts (Lira and Tororo) yet to receive IRS and drop five of the current IRS districts (Kitgum, Apac, Amuru, Lamwo, and Nwoya). When transitioning away from the five districts, PMI will ensure a stable supply of diagnostics and ACTs in addition to promotion of consistent and correct use of ITNs, and will provide support for monitoring and case surveillance following IRS withdrawal. PMI technical guidance/strategy for IRS will be used to help guide changes in the IRS and overall malaria prevention strategy in Uganda moving forward. Achievement of universal coverage could lead to less funding spent on IRS and transferring those cost-savings to support other critical programming such as improved case management and increased entomological and case surveillance. By ensuring good surveillance in areas in which IRS is being transitioned into/out of, PMI and NMCP can monitor the effects of these interventions, and make more informed programmatic decisions in the future. PMI will also initiate discussions with the NMCP about re-thinking the national IRS strategy given the cost of IRS and the anticipation of universal LLIN coverage.

Proposed PMI activities with FY 2014 funding: ($12,802,500)

PMI will support the NMCP to implement IRS in seven districts in Uganda, protecting approximately 2.6 million residents in these districts. A detailed spraying schedule starting in October 2014 is provided below (actual spray dates and order of spraying will be determined by ease of moving logistics, rain patterns, etc. at the time of spraying):

District	Spray Cycle	Spray Date
Gulu	Round 7	October 2014
Pader	Round 10	Oct-Nov 2014
Agago	Round 10	Oct-Nov 2014
Lira	Round 1	Oct-Nov 2014
Kole	Round 8	Nov-Dec 2014
Oyam	Round 8	Nov-Dec 2014
Tororo	Round 1	Nov-Dec 2014

Specific planned activities with FY 2014 funds are as follows:

- **Support for IRS:** PMI will continue to support IRS coverage in five of the ten districts that PMI has been spraying since 2009, and add two additional high burden districts. The districts that will no longer receive IRS will have a compensatory good case surveillance in place, as well as robust case management and promotion of ITNs. PMI will consider one or two additional high burden districts for IRS depending on actual spray costs at the time of implementation. PMI will support rotation from bendiocarb, a carbamate insecticide sprayed twice a year to the long-lasting organophosphate insecticide, pirimiphos-methyl, to which *An. gambiae* is completely susceptible in all areas of Uganda, reducing the yearly spray cycle from two to one spray cycles per year. The cost includes all components of IRS: insecticide procurement of long-lasting insecticide), spray pumps and other required logistics; environmental assessments; monitoring; and BCC activities specific to IRS. ($12,000,000)

- **Entomologic surveillance and monitoring:** PMI will continue to build local entomologic capacity by assisting the NMCP/Vector Control Division and Uganda Virus Research Institute at central and district levels including Gulu University to conduct comprehensive vector surveillance, including resistance surveys every two years; monthly insecticide decay rate monitoring; vector taxonomy on a small scale, and density and behavior studies done during entomological activities in bionomic studies to determine the resistance mechanism. Indicators will be measured in six locations targeted for IRS campaigns. Proposed entomological sentinel sites were selected on the basis of original six districts where each district has three sentinel sites representative of the whole project area covering ten districts. In addition to routine entomological monitoring activities in the project area we support an ongoing vector bionomics study being carried out monthly in two IRS districts and one non-IRS district where each district has two sentinel sites. Taking into account the newly developed PMI IRS guidelines, Uganda will explore ways of bringing down the number of sentinel sites to eight to ten in the IRS zone based on the number of houses and geographical location which would potentially reduce the cost per site. The cost of the proposed activities with FY 2014 funds will be approximately $60,000 per district (one site per district), which includes training, field costs, procurement of equipment, supplies, laboratory maintenance, and sample analysis. PMI will also support maintenance of two insectaries in collaboration with the Vector Control Division and Gulu University. ($600,000)

- **Develop local capacity to expand and sustain IRS:** Capacity development in the IRS project has covered two sectors: public sector including NMCP at the national and district level, and the private sector which includes pest control operators who can be potential IRS providers in future. Activities in this area cover training in IRS planning, implementation and monitoring and evaluation; entomological monitoring in IRS; and environmental compliance in IRS. PMI will continue to build the technical skills and capacity of the public sector as well as private sector, including companies and non-governmental organizations to oversee quality IRS programs, focusing on technical quality and accountability, in anticipation of future support for IRS through GOU and other stakeholders. Technical support will be given to NMCP, Vector Control Division and districts to plan, implement, manage, and monitor the technical quality of those IRS programs. ($150,000)

- **Entomology equipment and supplies:** In vector surveillance, insecticide resistance monitoring and laboratory supplies as needed by IRS implementing partner and NMCP. ($15,000)

- **3 TDYs from CDC-Atlanta**: CDC entomological staff will provide technical support for planning and monitoring IRS activities. This technical support covers testing for resistance mechanisms in *An. gambiae*, review of insectary maintenance and support for the PMI-funded insectary in Gulu, identification of *An. gambiae* sibling species in IRS district by polymerase chain reaction testing in Atlanta, and micro-analysis for transition planning. ($37,500)

INSECTICIDE-TREATED NETS

Background

The NMCP Strategic Plan for 2010/11-2014/15 outlines an objective of ensuring that at least 80% of the population consistently uses at least one malaria prevention method. This includes achieving and sustaining universal coverage with ITNs (defined as one net per two people in Uganda) and a strong, multi-pronged approach to increase usage. This complements PMI's targets of achieving 85% of all households owning at least one ITN and 85% of children under five years of age and pregnant women sleeping under an ITN every night.

Significant improvements in ITN ownership have occurred over the past several years as demonstrated in the ownership and usage statistics in the 2006, 2009, and 2011 national surveys. These improvements have been achieved through multiple partners' efforts, including PMI. The NMCP supports several strategies for net distribution: (1) commercial sale of ITNs at full cost; (2) sale of subsidized ITNs through the private sector; (3) free distribution to vulnerable groups through mass campaigns (targeting pregnant women and children under five years of age; HIV positive individuals usually receive nets through routine distribution through HIV treatment centers); and (4) free distribution through ANC/ EPI clinics. PMI provides ITN distribution through ANC clinics and has supported mass distribution in several districts. The Global Fund round 7 was expected to provide 17 million nets for universal coverage. At the end of Phase 1, in 2011, 7 million nets were received and distributed targeting pregnant women and children under five. These nets did not cover all districts and sub-counties. As a result, the proposed strategy is that the nets that will be received during the Phase 2 will be used to cover all households with one net for two people based on the registration data with total number of persons in each household. With the delayed implementation of Phase 2, there is a need for net replacement in households that received nets in Phase 1. The need for replacement of Phase 1 nets as well the population growth over the past four years have created additional gaps that must be covered under Phase 2. To fill this gap, DFID and PMI will be providing 5 million nets in 2013 to complement 15.5 nets anticipated from the Global Fund under Phase 2. In addition, distribution is already underway of 500,000 nets provided by World Vision in Soroti and Busia districts. This was completed in June 2013.

Sustained high coverage and use of ITNs in Uganda is a fundamental goal of the NMCP. ITN use has grown due to scale-up strategies focused primarily on catch-up coverage (mass distribution campaigns), followed by keep-up strategies mostly through continuous distribution schemes employing different approaches through a range of delivery channels. These strategies initially targeted only the highest risk populations of children under five and pregnant women. Recently, NMCP strives for universal coverage of the population in Uganda, aiming to reduce transmission overall—something that was not possible with the targeting of vulnerable groups.

Continuous distribution systems are crucial in maintaining the high coverage levels to be achieved by the universal coverage campaign. The national malaria control program in collaboration with RBM partners including PMI will support the expansion of continues distribution from two outlets (FANC and EPI) to four possible mechanisms (FANC and EPI, selected schools, and social marketing through commercial outlets). The regular supportive supervisions of the respective district health teams (DHTs) and PMI implementing partners M&E and NMCP/ M&E units will monitor the quality of ITNs distribution through continuous distribution channels.

PMI and other donors will be providing technical assistance to the NMCP as well as additional financial and material resources to support the net distribution campaign. PMI and other partners will also continue to support other BCC activities ensure appropriate use of nets at the household level.

Progress during the last 12 months

In FY 2012, PMI procured 1,200,000 ITNs and distributed approximately 220,000 of them through ANC clinics in the central, eastern, and western regions of the country. Approximately 650,000 ITNs were distributed in Bugiri, Kaliro, Serere, and Mayuge districts in eastern Uganda through mass campaigns to achieve universal coverage. A total of 1,619,227 people were registered in the four districts covering a total of 329,558 households. This included 418,634 children under five years of age and 56,431 pregnant women. All registered households received a net for every two people and a maximum of three nets when the household size is greater than six. However, the nets were not sufficient to cover all households. This initial distribution was intended to serve as a pilot of the distribution system that will be used for the planned Global Fund Phase 2 to achieve universal coverage.

Training on malaria in pregnancy, which includes education on the care, use, and benefits of nets resulted in 5,651 health workers trained in 2013, and the training will continue in 2014. PMI continued to support BCC to increase net usage through radio, health education at health facilities, through school programs and interpersonal communication at the community level.

Proposed PMI activities with FY 2014 funding: ($6,790,000)

With the planned 21 million nets from the Global Fund, PMI, DFID, and World Vision to be distributed in 2013, Uganda is expected to achieve universal coverage in 2014. Efforts to maintain coverage will be supported by PMI, including routine distribution through ANC which will complement the routine distribution planned through the Global Fund Round 10 grant. PMI will use the findings of the 2013/14 Malaria Consortium's pilot study (not funded by PMI) on continuous distribution in four eastern districts to provide guidance to the NMCP on potential alternative channels to maintain high ITN coverage in addition to ANC and EPI. The approach to be used will be defined in collaboration with the NMCP based on the findings of the pilot that will provide useful information for the development of an overall continuous distribution strategy for the country. In the Global Fund round 10 applications, there is a plan to distribute nets through ANC and EPI. PMI will distribute nets through ANC, EPI, schools, and commercial outlets as per the gap analysis presented. PMI will continue its efforts to increase correct and consistent net usage through BCC at the community, school and health facility levels. In addition, the findings from two evaluations on the culture of net use, care, and repair of nets will be incorporated into BCC activities to improve usage and longevity.

Major donors have not yet shared their contributions while having a gap of over 3 million ITN each year to maintain the achievements to be gained by the universal coverage, PMI as one of the lead malaria partners in Uganda will procure at least one third of the gap (1 million) each year until 2016.

ITNs Gap analysis

Year	2013	2014	2015	2016
Population	34,555,131	35,764,560	37,016,320	38,311,891
Coverage of net through Universal Coverage (UC) campaign	100%			
Total ITNs required for 2013 universal coverage (pop/1.8net)	19,197,295	-	-	-
Coverage of net through ANC	100%	100%	100%	100%
Number of ITNs required through ANC	1,727,757	1,788,228	1,850,816	1,915,595
Coverage of net through EPI	100%	100%	100%	100%
Number of ITNs required through EPI	1,382,205	1,430,528	1,480,653	1,532,475
Coverage of net through Social Marketing (2014-16)	-	pilot in two (TBD) PMI districts through 20 market outlets (1000/outlet)	through 40 market outlets (2000/outlet)	through 100 market outlets (2000/outlet)

Number of ITNs required through Social Marketing (2014-16)	-	20,000	80,000	200,000
Coverage of net through schools (2014-16)	-	pilot in four (TBD) PMI eastern districts through 20 schools (3000/school)	through 25 schools	through 30 schools
Number of ITNs required through Schools (2014-16)	-	60,000	75,000	90,000
Total nets required for UC and through the four outlets (ANC, EPI, Social marketing and schools) -**A**	22,307,257	3,298,756	3,486,469	3,738,070
Total ITNs funded for 2013 universal coverage by 1. PMI/DFID (5 million), 2. GF (15.5 million), and 3. World Vision (0.5 million)	21,000,000	-	-	-
ITNs funded by PMI/DFID through ANC (available for FY13 and projected for FY14-16)	549,800	1,000,000	1,000,000	1,000,000
ITNs funded by GF ANC/EPI	586,700	980,400	500,000	500,000
Total ITNs funded by donors and available for universal coverage, ANC/EPI 2013 and others (schools and social marketing 2014-16)-**B**	22,136,500	1,980,400	1,500,000	1,500,000
Gap (A-B)	170,757	1,318,356	1,986,469	2,238,070
Actual Gap (2013-2016)	**5,713,652**			

- **Procurement of ITNs:** PMI will procure approximately 1,000,000 ITNs for distribution through ANC clinics. Costs include the procurement, transportation, country clearances. and warehousing. ($4,900,000)

- **Distribution of free ITNs through ANC clinics:** PMI will target pregnant women for free distribution of 920,000 ITNs via ANC/EPI clinics in over 60 districts across Uganda. ($1,738,800)

- **Distribution of ITNs for free through 20 primary schools:** In four selected eastern districts 60,000 ITNs will be continuously available to be managed by one assigned school staff member in each school who provides ITNs according to specified criteria to be worked out. It may be: anyone who asks for one (i.e. acts as a source for the general population in areas where the population cannot afford or has no access to a commercial sector distributor), those who have a new baby at home, new school registrants, etc. Each target school distributes 3,000 ITNs per year. ($113,000)

- **Distribution of 20,000 ITNs through social marketing in the commercial sector such as shops and pharmacies:** The ITNs will be sold at a subsidized rate through existing but selected 20 market outlets (1,000 ITNs/ outlet per year). Costs can be set based on the spending power of the target group, which may be the general population. ($38,200)

- **BCC on net utilization:** Given the universal coverage net campaign underway and thus the high volume of ITNs to be distributed within one year, an enhanced BCC effort will be required to ensure appropriate and increased usage. In addition, the results from the two on-going studies on the culture of net use and care and repair of nets will be available in 2013 and will be incorporated into new BCC activities to improve usage and longevity of nets. With FY 2014 funds, PMI will support community, school, and health facility level BCC activities. (BCC activities funds are included in the distribution costs mentioned above).

MALARIA IN PREGNANCY

Background

The 2012 MOH National Malaria Control Policy provides guidance on management of malaria in pregnancy. Pregnant women should be treated with the most effective antimalarial medicine under medical supervision. Pregnant women who present with fever are tested for malaria using either microscopy or RDT, and treated for malaria if the test results are positive. Those with negative test results are also treated for malaria if there is no other known cause of fever. Oral quinine is used for treatment of uncomplicated malaria in pregnancy in the first trimester, and ACT is used in the second and third trimester. Parenteral artesunate or quinine is used to treat severe malaria in pregnancy in the first, second, and third trimester.

The objectives of the National Malaria Control Policy to guide implementation of malaria in pregnancy programs are:

1. To ensure every pregnant woman sleeps under an ITN throughout her pregnancy and thereafter.

2. To ensure pregnant women receive IPTp with an appropriate medicine and receive early diagnosis and prompt management of malaria episodes.

Uganda's policy is aligned to new WHO guidance that IPTp should be given at every ANC visit starting second trimester if not given in the prior four weeks. IPTp is integrated with and is operationalized through the Reproductive Health Unit FANC policy which recommends that women with a normal pregnancy make four visits to an ANC clinic prior to delivery.

Currently, there is no established threshold level of malaria transmission below which IPTp with sulfadoxine-pyrimethamine (SP) is no longer cost-effective and should therefore be suspended. However, monitoring of IPTp-SP effectiveness is essential and should continue. The most recent WHO guideline advises that SP should be administered with 0.4 mg per day of folic acid, and that folic acid at a daily dose equal or above 5 mg should not be given concomitantly with SP as this counteracts its efficacy as an antimalarial.

The 2011 Uganda Malaria Program Review reported the need for full integration of the IPTp program within the Reproductive Health Unit, leaving the NMCP with the responsibility of providing technical assistance to the Reproductive Health Unit to ensure quality IPTp implementation, including training of health workers on IPTp, ensuring that provision of IPTp services at health facilities follows directly observed therapy, supportive supervision, M&E, operational research, and BCC campaigns at the community level for IPTp. The Reproductive Health Unit is now the focal point for IPTp implementation and activities are integrated within the FANC policy and procedures.

Antenatal attendance by pregnant women in Uganda remains high, with 2011 DHS results showing > 95% of pregnant women made at least one ANC visit while only 25% attended at least two times. PMI in collaboration with other partners have made various efforts to ensure the availability of SP at health facilities, provision of water and cups at the ANC clinics for directly observed treatment (DOT) of SP and training of health workers. However, the 2011 DHS shows low IPTp uptake. Multiple hypotheses have been used to explain the low coverage rates of IPTp, including unwillingness of some pregnant women to take SP because they are not aware of the need for malaria prevention in pregnancy, fear of its effect on the fetus (a fear sometimes fostered by health workers);[10] negligence of midwives not giving SP to pregnant women, SP stockouts, and irregular ANC attendance by pregnant women;[11] however, the reasons for low IPTp uptake need further exploration.

---

[10] Barker J, Payes R, (2007). "Overview of Programmatic Interventions for Communication for Indoor Residual Spraying (IRS), Insecticide-treated Nets (ITNs), Case Management and malaria in Pregnancy." USAID.

[11] Ndyomugyenyi R and Katamanywa J. 2010. Intermittent preventive treatment of malaria in pregnancy (IPTp): do frequent antenatal care visits ensure access and compliance to IPTp in Ugandan rural communities? *Trans R Soc Trop Med Hyg.*

In light of the low uptake of IPTp2 observed nationally, Malaria Consortium is conducting a study to assess barriers to uptake of two courses of intermittent preventive treatment of malaria in pregnancy. The project aims to (1) determine which barriers may still pose challenges to IPTp uptake in Uganda, and identify new barriers, with a focus on: barriers to receiving a first dose of SP as part of focused antenatal care (FANC) and barriers to receiving a second dose of SP as part of FANC for women who have already received one dose, (2) develop a set of recommendations, including a potential intervention, which will improve uptake of IPTp2 and enable the Uganda NMCP to meet the goal of 85% coverage of IPTp2. This study is in very early stages. Results are expected to be available in early 2014.

Progress during the last 12 months

During the past year, as part of an integrated approach, PMI has supported monitoring of SP stock levels in health facilities to help maintain adequate SP supplies for IPTp. Stock data results were discussed with the NMCP to enable their advocacy for replenishment of the supply at the National Medical Stores (NMS), when necessary. PMI supported on-the-job mentorship to health facility staff during integrated supportive supervision conducted to promote IPTp directly observed treatment (DOT) and increase the uptake of IPTp2. During the last year, PMI continued to procure and distribute safe drinking water commodities including cups and jerry cans for IPTp to health facilities in 34 target districts including distributing 1,700 cups and 170 jerry cans to health facilities.

PMI has continued to provide support for IPTp which has resulted in the development of a comprehensive malaria in pregnancy module incorporated into the FANC training. PMI supported the training and on-the-job supervision of 5,651 health workers in integrated management of malaria including malaria in pregnancy. In collaboration with PEPFAR, PMI has supported integrating IPTp within prevention of mother to child transmission services and extended this support to private not-for-profit health facilities. PMI also supported integration of malaria in pregnancy activities within district-based efforts aimed at strengthening FANC.

PMI supported strengthening of private health sector capacity to implement malaria in pregnancy interventions according to national guidelines. These activities were targeted at providers working in "Good Life Clinics and Good Life Shops", a private sector franchise model of health care delivery. In the five PMI districts 250 health care providers from 131 private health facilities were trained (36 private clinics, 95 drug shops). PMI's support to ensure pregnant women have access to and sleep under ITNs is outlined under the ITN section above.

Proposed PMI activities with FY 2014 funding: ($650,000)

With FY 2014 funds, PMI will continue to support strengthening the delivery of malaria in pregnancy services including increasing the uptake of IPTp in both the public and private sectors. Activities will include support for continued integration of strengthened malaria in pregnancy services into FANC and prevention of mother to child transmission (PEPFAR) platforms. PMI will continue to support promotion of correct and consistent use of ITNs distributed through the universal coverage campaign and during ANC visits. Once results are available from the study evaluating factors contributing to low IPTp uptake, PMI will work with the NMCP and partners to implement the findings and recommendations. With FY 2014 funds, PMI will also support the Reproductive Health Unit and the NMCP to establish an MIP technical working group to ensure implementation of the recent revised WHO IPTp guidance.

Specifically, with FY 2014 funds PMI will:

- **Provide support for strengthening delivery of comprehensive IPTp services as part of integrated FANC at public ANC clinics:** Based on previous PMI support for IPTp services and results from the uptake evaluation, PMI will continue to support a package of services to maximize IPTp provision. This will include: support for procurement of SP, provision of clean water and cups to facilitate directly observed treatment of IPTp; provision of ANC registers for medical records; enhanced BCC to support district health education units to ensure that pregnant women understand that IPTp is safe and the importance of completing a full course of IPTp; and community-level advocacy to encourage pregnant women to attend ANC. PMI will also assist with integrated supervision for ANC health workers (with emphasis on IPTp, ITNs, and case management of pregnant women). PMI will support selected professional associations for health talks through radio and TV to improve the attitude of ANC attendants (midwives, nurses, and doctors) for more communication during antenatal visits. PMI will support integration of service delivery with prevention of mother to child transmission of HIV in facilities where this service is provided and will continue to strengthen integrated programs for maternal and child health. ($550,000)

- **Provide support for comprehensive IPTp services at ANC clinics in the private-for-profit sector:**

    o Even though PMI mainly supports the public sector, a considerable number of pregnant women who are willing and able to pay visit private-for- profit facilities due to better attitude of providers, proximity and availability of services on demand. PMI will continue to promote IPTp through training of health workers in small to medium-sized private sector health clinics in order to enable them to promote a comprehensive package for IPTp, early detection of malaria during pregnancy, and offer directly observed treatment. PMI will strengthen private health sector capacity in implementing the national malaria strategic plan in the management of malaria in pregnancy at private health facilities. These funds will also support BCC for ANC clients seeking care at private facilities and allow PMI to leverage on-going support from PEPFAR and MCH funds for private sector. ($100,000)

    o BCC: See Cross-cutting BCC section for details on activities and funding.

Malaria Diagnosis

Background

The current National Malaria Control Policy, adopted in 2012, recommends parasite-based diagnosis with microscopy or RDTs as part of malaria case management in all health facilities and at the community level for all age groups. The policy states that:

1. Suspected malaria cases will be subjected to parasite-based diagnosis.
2. Microscopy remains the "reference or gold standard" for malaria diagnosis in case management and shall be the diagnostic method of choice for all health centers level III (that have microscopes) and above.
3. RDTs will be used at health center III's without microscopes, health center II's and community level and to fill the gaps at higher level health facilities where microscopy is not possible.
4. The type of RDTs to be deployed in the country will be guided by evidence on sensitivity, specificity, ease of use and stability in the field, as determined by the performance evaluation and pre-qualification schemes of the WHO coupled with in-country testing. Currently Uganda is using CareStart Malaria HRP II (Pf).

This is consistent with WHO guidance on the need for parasitological confirmation of fevers in all groups before treatment with antimalarial drugs.[12] To achieve this policy directive, PMI has been working closely with NMCP and other partners to ensure there is adequate equipment and supplies for microscopy at the higher level health facilities and RDTs at the lower levels. Elaborate plans have also been developed to support country-wide training of personnel on both microscopy and RDTs. These efforts have contributed to the training of at least one health worker in either microscopy or RDT use in more than 70% of districts across the country. Uganda is a beneficiary of both AMFm and Round 10 Global Fund grants. In both grants, significant resources have been committed to provide RDTs for malaria. The first tranche of approximately 14 million RDTs through AMFm support arrived in country December 2012, a supply which should cover all public sector needs for at least one calendar year. The table below is from the Global Fund Round 10 proposal and provides a gap analysis of the RDT needs for the country in 2014. The RDT gap analysis assumes a contribution of 1 million RDTs from PMI. The Global Fund grant Round 10 is expected to procure 11 million RDTs. The Uganda NMCP strategic plan 2010/11 – 2014/2015 has an ambitious plan that aims to achieve 90% testing of all fever cases by 2015. However, it is projected that with increasing availability of RDTs for laboratory confirmation and the completion of training scheduled by the Stop Malaria Project, there is a possibility of achieving 70% diagnostic confirmation of fever cases.

---

[12] WHO. 2010. Guidelines for the treatment of malaria -- 2nd edition. 1. Malaria – drug therapy. 2. Malaria – diagnosis. 3. Antimalarials – administration and dosage. 4. Drug therapy, Combination. 5. Guidelines. I. World Health Organization.

The Global Fund Round 10 Proposal Gap Analyses for RDT

	2013	2014	2015	2016
Total no. suspected malaria cases from health facility data- 44% of patients visiting a PNFP & Public health facility (MIS, 2009)	45,317,945	46,904,073	48,545,715	50,244,815
% decrease in suspected malaria cases with vector control	15%	15%	15%	15%
Reduction in number of suspected malaria cases	6,797, 692	7,035,611	7,281,857	7,536,722
Total number of malaria cases after vector control	38,520,253	39,868,462	41,263,858	42,708,093
% target cases subjected to parasitological diagnosis test under this proposal	55%	70%	80%	80%
Number of diagnoses required	21,186,139	27,907,923	33,011,086	34,166,474
Microscopy (to be used at 80% of HCIII, 100% of HCIV & Hospitals)	31%	40%	45%	45%
Microscopy slides	12,045,508	15,867,219	18,768,654	19,425,557
RDTs (to be used at 20% of HCIII, 100% of HII & Community)	24%	30%	35%	35%
RDTs	9,140, 631	12,040,704	14,242,433	14,740,918
Available RDTs	1,000,000	1,000,000	1,000,000	1,000,000
Gap in RDT need	8,140,631	11,040,704	13,242,433	13,740,918
GF request (50% of need in 2010 and 2016)	8,140,631	11,040,704	13,242,433,	6,870,459
Total quantity requested over the 5- year period				45,245,054

ASSUMPTIONS: 1) Consumption data of the number of unconfirmed malaria cases seen in public and PNFP health facilities reported to the HMIS for the last 3 years were extrapolated to account for reporting rates of 80%. Data were extrapolated taking into account that 44% of fever patient's access treatment through public/PNFP facilities (UMIS 2009) to produce an estimate of the total number suspected malaria cases country wide. **2)** The target number of malaria cases to be treated through the community & public/PNFP health facilities and at community level is 80% by 2015 **3)** A 5% reduction in suspected malaria cases is factored in for 2011, the year after universal coverage with LLINs is achieved. Further reductions of 10% and 15% are expected in 2012 and 2013. The projected reductions are based on the assumption that approximately 50% of suspected malaria cases are parasitologically confirmed as malaria, hence the rate of reduction of suspected malaria cases will only decrease at half the rate of confirmed malaria cases **4)** Microscopy will contribute to 45% of all diagnosis by 2015 and will be implemented at all hospitals, all HC IVs and all HC IIIs by 2012. RDTS will contribute to 35% of diagnosis of all malaria cases by 2015 and will be deployed at HC IIIs, all HC IIs and community level. **5)** The remaining 20% of malaria cases will be treated under the private sector. **6)** The gaps from 2011-2015 will be covered by this proposal. **7)** The number of health facilities with microscopes will increase through the previous TB grant and under the HSS section.

The new diagnostic policy has been rolled out in all public health facilities in the country. However, adherence to the policy is still suboptimal with most malaria diagnosis still based on clinical symptoms. PMI observed during site visits, meetings, and facility record reviews, that there is limited awareness and/or willingness on both the clinician and patient sides to request and adhere to testing prior to treatment. Clinicians also need to be re-oriented on the possible differential diagnosis of fever when the malaria laboratory test is negative. This is in addition to many facilities lacking adequate laboratory diagnostic capacity, especially laboratory technicians. The 2009 MIS found that only 17% of children with a fever were tested for malaria before receiving treatment, and the average laboratory confirmation reported in the 2009 National HMIS was 24% (amongst all age groups). The DHS 2011 shows an increase to 24.7% for children with fever that were tested for malaria before receiving treatment. As malaria prevention activities are scaled up, in particular the universal ITN distribution planned to finish early 2014, appropriate diagnosis and treatment will become even more critical because malaria is not the sole cause of fevers and health workers will need to diagnose and treat other causes of fever. Future efforts will require sustained education of clinicians and other cadre of health staff to base treatment on the test results and to educate communities to demand a malaria test before receiving antimalarial treatment.

The Central Public Health Laboratory (CPHL) is mandated to coordinate, monitor, and supervise all health center III and IV laboratories, but is grossly understaffed and supervision is irregular. PMI and PEPFAR will continue their collaboration in laboratory strengthening by supporting CPHL and NMCP to conduct regular supervision of facilities for sustained quality diagnostic services.

As with any laboratory test, a comprehensive quality assurance program is critical to the provision of accurate, timely test results. Furthermore, as clinicians and patients become increasingly dependent upon diagnostic tests in management of malaria and febrile illness, it becomes more important that malaria microscopy and rapid diagnostic testing services are of consistently high quality, and that clinicians and patients can confidently rely upon laboratory results for patient care decisions. A quality assurance/quality control (QA/QC) system for diagnostics is being developed by the NMCP with support from PMI and other partners.

Progress during the last 12 months

In the last year, PMI supported the NMCP to update the country's guidelines for diagnosis with microscopy and RDTs. Importantly, these guidelines (to be finalized by 2014) specifically recognize the necessity of supporting both the public and private sector, in order to increase the proportion of suspected malaria cases receiving testing prior to treatment.

PMI supported trainings that demonstrated significantly increased knowledge and skills after the training. PMI partners have trained 294 health workers in the use of rapid diagnostic tests in three districts and 1,471 technicians in malaria microscopy. The pre-and post-test results of the training showed a tremendous improvement in the accuracy in diagnosis of malaria. During the previous year, as an example, the ability of laboratory personnel to correctly read slides improved in Rukungiri District, from 83% to 94%. Several trainers conducted joint follow-up support supervision visits six weeks after completion of the microscopy training. During these visits, the team assessed health workers' competence in performing and interpreting test results, treatment for negative and positive patients, and records management and assessment. The results showed improvement in case management. Supervision team members also provided on-the-job training, and collected data to assess the effects of the training on the overall management of fever cases.

In addition to capacity building on diagnostics, PMI has supported the PNFP facilities with RDTs to improve access to diagnostics. In 2011, PMI supported Joint Medical Stores in storing and distributing nearly 1 million RDTs. This support includes capacity building on supply chain management with a focus on consumption data and forecasting.

With support from PMI, a quality assurance manual that outlines the plan for implementing a pilot district level malaria microscopy quality assurance program in Uganda has been developed. It encompasses retraining, validation and the development of competency standards designed to ensure the quality of diagnosis necessary for a successful malaria program, while remaining within the expected financial and personnel resource constraints.

PMI funding has supported a pilot of a quality assurance program for microscopy in select districts with blood smears from health facilities (previously trained with PMI support), being cross checked at both district and national level. Slide cross-checking is time-consuming and the problem is compounded by lack of trained staff at the facility level. Current pilot efforts therefore rely on slide re-checking by expert microscopists at the central level who provide feedback to the periphery microscopists through supportive supervision.

PMI supported supportive supervisions in all focus health facilities once every three months. During support supervision, on-site mentorship is provided to the laboratory staff to strengthen their skills on-job and to correct any deficiencies identified through slide cross-checking.

Proposed PMI activities with FY 2014 funding: ($2,222,500)

With FY 2014 funds, PMI will support QA/QC and provide supportive supervision to health workers to improve parasite-based diagnosis at all levels of the health system and in both public and private facilities. PMI and NMCP will work closely with WHO and CDC PMI to support the development of an appropriate quality assurance and control system. PMI support will complement Global Fund and PEFPAR funding for general laboratory and microscopy strengthening and PMI will work with PEPFAR to improve coordination of USG efforts to improve the laboratory system in Uganda. Specifically, with FY 2014 funds PMI will support:

- **Diagnostics supplies procurement:** PMI will continue to procure about 850,000 RDTs targeted at filling gaps in the national coverage for diagnostics. ($610,000)

- **Support QA/QC and supportive supervision for diagnostics at health centers**: Together with a new malaria-specific mechanism (TBD), the Mission's integrated regional programs will increase the geographical coverage of health services, including malaria services. PMI will support case management trainings that focus on appropriate diagnosis, QA/QC, and supportive supervision for diagnostics. ($1,550,000)

- **Support improved diagnostics in the for-profit private sector:** PMI will support training on the use of RDTs, supervision and quality assurance (for both RDTs and microscopy) in the for profit corporate private sector through existing partnerships with 55 companies through the 1:1 matching contribution program for malaria (fifteen participating companies currently). ($50,000)

- **TDY from CDC-Atlanta**: CDC staff will provide technical support to laboratory diagnostics support of the QA/QC policy. ($12,500)

Malaria Treatment

Background

Since 2004, AL has been the first-line treatment for uncomplicated malaria in Uganda. The second-line treatments are dihydroartemisinin-piperaquine (DP) and quinine. Artesunate suppositories are recommended for pre-referral treatment of severe malaria at the community level where parenteral therapy is not possible. The National Malaria Control Policy continues to recommend AL as first-line treatment (with artesunate/amodiaquine as an alternative first-line), and recently adopted WHO guidance to introduce parenteral artesunate for treatment of severe malaria.

The supply of ACTs at health facilities has improved over time with the increase in commodity availability and changes in the national system of supplying the facilities. A survey done in four districts two years after the beginning of the new policy implementation revealed that there are often stockouts of the recommended drugs (13% of the facilities reported complete lack of AL in the past 2 weeks); however, this has drastically improved due to increased availability of ACTs from AMFm and purchases with GOU's own resources from Quality Chemical Industries Limited, a local manufacturer that recently obtained WHO approval for ACTs. In addition, some facilities are still benefitting from the "push-kit" system of drug supplies whereby NMS provides a specified quantity of drugs to health centers II and III every two months. The improved supply of ACTs through these efforts has greatly reduced ACT stockouts at health facilities. The push-kit, however, does not take into account the actual needs of individual health facilities, thus some facilities do end up with stockouts, while others have an oversupply. Efforts by the district MOH and PMI partners have been made to redistribute supplies in these cases as well as document the under- and over-supply to assist NMS in revising the contents of the kits. The improved supply of ACTs in public facilities has been evidenced by 44% of children with fever reporting use of ACTs in the results of the 2011 DHS, a substantial increase from the 14% of children reported by the 2009 MIS.

Although intravenous (IV) artesunate is now recommended for treatment of severe malaria, the MOH is still trying to develop a plan for a sustained supply of artesunate, which is likely to be phased in over the next several years. Intravenous quinine continues to be used for treatment of severe malaria during this transition; unfortunately improper administration of quinine frequently occurs due to inadequate supplies of IV dextrose solutions, and may lead to overdosing patients.

In line with the malaria treatment policy, in 2006 the Ministry of Health introduced use of ACTs for HBMF in 40 out of 80 old districts. There has been piecemeal implementation of HBMF with ACTs, and scale-up has never been countrywide due to an inadequate supply of ACTs. With funding from the Global Fund, training on implementation of HBMF using ACTs was rolled out to 39 more districts in 2010. Building on the success of the HBMF strategy and in order to facilitate access to and reduce treatment gap for malaria, pneumonia and diarrhea, the MOH together with development partners in July 2010 adopted a strategy for Integrated Community Case Management (iCCM) for these diseases. The iCCM program includes using AL to treat malaria, oral trimethoprim-sulfamethoxazole or amoxicillin to treat pneumonia and oral rehydration solution and zinc for diarrhea at the community level. However, repeated shortages of AL, challenges with motivating community volunteers, and poor referral systems from community to health facilities have hampered implementation. Another challenge has been the different funding streams supporting HBMF and iCCM resulting in differences in implementation of these programs. The HBMF strategy was funded through Global Fund, and iCCM through the Canadian International Development Agency and the Gates Foundation. The iCCM funding is for a two-year pilot in 20 districts and provides funding for training on case management and drug supplies to the village health teams (VHTs) only (i.e. there is no provision of drugs to health facilities who are the referral and supervisory points of contact for the VHTs). While the Global Fund Round 10 grant does merge HBMF with iCCM, its support is for 31 districts only, and there is no guarantee continued of support for the districts that have rolled iCCM out already. In December 2012, the pilot phase started to be evaluated. Preliminary results are positive, and include a drastic increase in children receiving prompt ACT treatment (from 8 to 45%). Based on these results and the identified gap in increasing access to prompt treatment, PMI will reinstitute support for iCCM in a few districts in FY 2014 in the USAID malaria project integrated health projects. It will be very important to perform a cost-benefit analysis of iCCM in its current context to ensure that the current iCCM policy is the most appropriate use of resources.

Delivery of healthcare services in Uganda is predominantly through the private sector. A recent assessment found that there are 5,500 health facilities in Uganda: 49% are private for profit clinics, 13% are PNFP, and 38% are public facilities all levels. Care seeking is heavily focused in the private sector with up to 82% of households first seeking care from small drug shops, private clinics, and private-not-for-profit providers.[13] Results from the 2009 MIS also highlight the importance of the private sector in the provision of care; 55% of children with fever received care at private facilities. In the last two years, PMI extended its support to the PNFP facilities. In 2011, PMI supported the procurement of 3.3 million ACT treatments and 934,000 RDTs and a controlled system of distribution of ACTs to PNFP facilities is currently underway through the Joint Medical Store (JMS). This was a critical intervention, given that the previous arrangement in which NMS provided 20% of the public supply of ACTs to PNFP facilities through JMS has ceased. PMI supported training of private health practitioners in the new antimalarial drug policy. This training is often integrated with sessions on HIV/AIDS, family planning, and child survival. To date, nearly 7,000 private health practitioners have received training in malaria treatment and prevention. In addition, PMI has supported small-to-medium sized private clinics and has worked with large private corporations to leverage additional funds for malaria prevention through their Corporate Social Responsibility programs. These corporations provide free or subsidized health services to their employees and the surrounding communities. PMI works with these businesses on a cost-sharing basis for ITNs, IPTp, and laboratory diagnostics.

Quality of care in both public and private health facilities needs additional support and improvement. A PMI-supported health facility assessment showed that the clinical evaluation of patients presenting with fever is sub-optimal as evidenced by poor history taking, incomplete examination of such children, with few clinicians looking for danger signs. In addition the clinicians often did not provide an explanation of the diagnosis, treatment, and follow up.[14] Another evaluation on treatment practices for severe malaria in east and mid-western Uganda showed a considerable gap in quality of care: with delays in prompt care (received in only 29% of patients); correct diagnosis of severe malaria in only 27% of patients; and appropriate administration of quinine in the correct volume of 5% dextrose in 18% of patients, with 80% of patients receiving more than one dose of quinine in one single bottle of dextrose.[15] There is still a considerable amount of work to be done to improve quality of care for patients with malaria. PMI has been addressing these aspects of quality care through implementation of support supervision, clinical audits, and training.

Progress during the last 12 months

During the past year, PMI has procured more than 1 million ACT treatments and trained more than 5,000 health facility workers in case management of malaria with ACTs. In addition, PMI supported the NMCP in the development of a training curriculum for integrated management of malaria which includes management of both uncomplicated and severe malaria (with proper administration of IV artesunate); management of malaria in pregnancy and parasite-based diagnosis with RDTs (including how to manage a patient with a negative RDT and fever). PMI supported training of health workers at all health facility levels in 34 districts. The Joint Uganda Malaria Program Training (JUMP) curriculum was expanded to develop the current integrated malaria management training curriculum to implement training in the whole country.

---

[14] STOP Malaria Project, September 2011. *Health Facility Assessment Survey Report* (unpublished).

[15] Achan J, Tibenderana J, Kyabayinze D, Mawejje H, Mugizi R, et al. (2011) *Case Management of Severe Malaria - A Forgotten Practice: Experiences fromHealth Facilities in Uganda*. PLoS ONE 6(3): e17053. doi:10.1371/journal.pone.0017053

To ensure adherence to the new policy changes and appropriate management of patients with malaria, the MoH is building the capacity of health workers in diagnosis (clinical and laboratory), treatment and prevention of malaria. The MoH is implementing the training in integrated malaria management and is in the process of dissemination of comprehensive, up-to-date information regarding facility based management of malaria. The integrated malaria management training course seeks to promote proper management of patients with fever by advocating for improved evaluation and treatment of patients with fever. This course also aims at creating team spirit among health facility staff for effective management of patients with fever. Emphasis is also put on educating patients so that they adopt malaria preventive practices. A team of national trainers was trained and they in turn have trained regional trainers. The regional trainers are in the process of rolling out the training to all the districts with support from the national trainers.

Proposed PMI activities with FY 2014 funding: ($3,845,000)

With FY 2014 funds, PMI will continue to support strengthening case management activities of uncomplicated and severe malaria including procuring commodities that will be distributed to PNFP facilities through JMS. Given the positive results of the iCCM pilot project, the improved supply of ACTs in health facilities, and the finding that approximately 75% of Ugandans live within five kilometers of a health facility,[16] PMI will prioritize strengthening clinical services at health facility levels, while supporting implementation of iCCM in a few districts in northern Uganda.

Planned activities with FY 2014 funds are as follows:

- **Procure antimalarial drugs**: PMI will support the procurement of drugs including ACTs (artemether-lumefantrine – AL) and severe malaria drugs (IV artesunate) for the treatment of malaria. The planned ACT and RDT procurement (the latter is mentioned in the Diagnostics section) is targeted for the PNFP sector through JMS, while the drugs for severe malaria will be for both PNFP and public sector. ($1,500,000)

- **Support private sector providers and their networks to strengthen malaria case management and increase the role of district health officials in providing support and supervision**: PMI will continue supporting private clinics and drug shops that are the closest sources of care for children with fever in many communities. This support includes enhancing collaboration between the public sector district health teams with the private sector associations to ensure that clinicians and drug owners receive routine supportive supervision for proper clinical care of children with fever, including treatment based on parasitological diagnosis, and support improvements in record keeping and HMIS reporting to national level. ($332,500)

- **Strengthen case management in health facilities**: PMI will provide funds for strengthening case management, including parasitological diagnosis of uncomplicated

---

[16] Ministry of Health (MOH) [Uganda] and Macro International Inc. 2008. *Uganda Service Provision Assessment Survey 2007*. Kampala, Uganda: Ministry of Health and Macro International Inc.

and severe malaria in public, and private not-for-profit (faith- based) health facilities in most of parts of Uganda. This support includes clinical audits, support supervision, in-service training and iCCM in select pilot districts, enhancing collaboration between NMCP and the national professional councils (doctors, nurses, midwives, laboratory technologist/technicians, and pharmacists), in order to strengthen case management. PMI will also provide funds for strengthening collaboration between district health teams and district-level professional associations to promote correct diagnosis, and early and prompt treatment. PMI will support pre and in-service training, supportive supervision, and provision of job-aids to health care workers. ($2,000,000)

- **TDY from CDC-Atlanta**: CDC staff will provide technical support to quality of care issues for the management of severe and uncomplicated malaria within PMI and NMCP programs. ($12,500)

Pharmaceutical Management

Background

While the pharmaceutical management system in Uganda remains weak, there have been significant improvements in recent years; especially in the supply of ACTs at district and lower level health facilities, as outlined in the Case Management section above.

NMS is responsible for procuring and supplying supplies to the public sector, while JMS is the officially recognized supplier for private-not-for-profit facilities (faith- based non-governmental organization run facilities). National ACT supplies have been more stable in the last 24 months due to procurements from the Global Fund, DFID and the GOU, while the "push kit" introduced by the MOH and NMS two years ago has helped to ensure that there is at least some stocks of ACTs routinely available at all lower level public health facilities. . The push-kit, however, does not take into account the actual needs of individual health facilities, thus some facilities do end up with stockouts, while others have an oversupply. Efforts by the district MOH and PMI partners have been made to redistribute supplies in these cases as well as document the under- and over-supply to assist NMS in revising the contents of the kits. More than a year ago, NMS also began direct "last mile" distribution to the health facilities they cover using private sector third party logistics providers.

Quality of antimalarial drugs is a concern worldwide and Uganda, through the National Drug Authority (NDA), conducts quality control at ports of entry but also post-marketing surveillance. Multiple partners provide support for these processes including PMI, through a wider USAID partnership and the Global Fund.

Progress during the last 12 months

PMI continues to provide technical assistance at national down through peripheral health facility levels to help the NMS, the NMCP, and district health programs to improve their quantification of AL, RDTs, SP for IPTp and severe malaria drugs. Greater progress has been seen in the past twelve to twenty-four months in ensuring stable supplies at health facility levels particularly in improving stock management and reporting. With FY 2012 funding, PMI provided significant support to strengthening the supply chain management system in the PNFP sector including an assessment of logistics management capabilities and on-job training of staff in more than 500 facilities; development of an ACT and RDT ordering and reporting system (for web-based and manual orders), and establishment of a distribution system to diocese headquarters for malaria commodities. This was the first time such work was carried out in the PNFP sector. The data from facility reports is enabling PMI to forecast ACT and RDT requirements for the PNFP sector with much greater accuracy. Both the work in the public and PNFP facilities is done through a larger USAID Uganda partner and leverages the wider program to build capacity and improve performance of the national health supply chain system. PMI supported an End-Use Verification survey in 20 randomly selected health facilities in four districts to determine the extent to which antimalarials were available to the end-user and how effective supply chain systems were used in managing malaria commodities in late 2012. The End-Use Verification survey showed that facility order and delivery documentation was only available in seven out of 20 sampled facilities. The absence of this documentation makes it impossible for facilities to crosscheck delivery versus ordered quantities contributing to the risk of stockouts. There remains much opportunity for strengthening national NMS procurement, quantification, supply management, and documentation where systems remain particularly weak.

PMI's supports strengthening the NDA through an integrated health sector program that focuses on improving their strategy and capability in information management as well as their quality control and inspection programs. Support for post-market surveillance, testing of medicines already in the market and also at entry points continues and with PMI support, scanning equipment (True-scan) was procured enabling testing of malaria and other essential medicines.

The increased and targeted testing has already highlighted the magnitude of the problem of medicines' quality. While the percentage of sampled essential medicines failing NDA quality test between 2009/2010 and 2010/2011 decreased from 18% failure rate to 10%, the failure rate for malaria medicines increased from 7% to 22%.[17]

Proposed PMI activities with FY 2014 funding: ($400,000)

- **Strengthen pharmaceutical supply chain management and monitor drug quality of antimalarials**: PMI will continue to provide technical assistance to the NMCP/MOH to forecast national requirements for essential medicines and coordinate national supply planning among the various suppliers. Malaria specific activities include: Forecasting and quantification of malaria commodity needs including ACTs, SP, RDTs and other antimalarial medicines; reporting on these commodities when provided to the private-not-for-profit sector; and supporting monitoring of ACT stockouts in all facilities. Support

---

[17] PMP indicators for SURE indicator 2.22 and 2.23, 2012 report.

will also continue to JMS to continue monitoring and improving the ordering and distribution system for PMI-procured ACTs and RDTs. In addition, support will be provided at district and health facility levels to strengthen the lower level supply chain. Support to NDA will continue to improve their quality control activities of priority and high risk medicines, including antimalarial drugs, supplied to the country. The PMI investment in supply chain management leverages more than $5 million from other health funding streams (including PEPFAR) to strengthen the entire supply chain system. ($400,000)

Drug Resistance Monitoring

Background

In 2004, the first-line therapy was changed to ACT, with AL adopted as first-line and amodiaquine plus artesunate (AQ+AS) as an alternative drug. Quinine was recommended as the second-line treatment. During 2005 and 2006, the NMCP implemented the new treatment policy by revising national malaria case-management guidelines, in-service training for health workers, and provision of AL to government, and private-not-for-profit health facilities. AL is delivered to the facilities in four standard weight-specific blister packages, each containing a different number of the same strength tablets and is provided free of charge. However, ensuring availability and proper use of the recommended drugs at all facilities countrywide has proven to be a challenge. Recently however studies in Cambodia have shown increased resistance of parasite isolates and reduced efficacy to different artemisinin derivatives. As resistance to ACTs is emerging in Asia, monitoring drug resistance is critical. Studies on the development of resistance to ACT and the spread of ACT-resistant parasite strains in the population are therefore extremely relevant from a public health perspective.

Since 2001, Uganda has monitored first-line antimalarials and PMI has supported this work since 2006. As of 2009, evidence showed that all formulations of ACTs tested were still highly effective.[18] [19] Studies conducted in 2006 and 2009 have compared AL, amodiaquine, artesunate and dihydroartemisinin-piperaquine. PMI together with WHO are supporting a round of drug efficacy monitoring evaluating the efficacy and safety of two ACTs, amodiaquine-artesunate (AQ+AS), and AL for treatment of uncomplicated malaria in children in Uganda.

---

[18] The Four Artemisinin-Based Combinations (4ABC) Study Group (2011) *A Head-to-Head Comparison of Four Artemisinin-Based Combinations for Treating Uncomplicated Malaria in African Children: A Randomized Trial.* PLoS Med 8(11): e1001119. doi:10.1371/journal.pmed.1001119

[19] Emmanuel Arinaitwe,Taylor G. Sandison Humphrey Wanzira, Abel Kakuru, Jaco Homsy, Julius Kalamya, Moses R. Kamya,Neil Vora,Bryan Greenhouse, Philip J. Rosenthal,Jordan Tappero, and Grant Dorsey. *"Artemether-Lumefantrine versus Dihydroartemisinin-Piperaquine for Falciparum Malaria: A Longitudinal, Randomized Trial in Young Ugandan Children,"* Clinical Infectious Diseases 2009; 49:1629–37

Progress during the last 12 months

PMI has supported monitoring of antimalarial treatment efficacy of the first-line antimalarials in Uganda. A study comparing the efficacy and safety of amodiaquine-artesunate (AQ+AS), and AL for treatment of uncomplicated malaria in children in Uganda is ongoing with results expected in late 2013.

Proposed PMI activities with FY 2014 funding:

- **Monitor drug quality of antimalarials:** To ensure all antimalarials entering the Uganda market are of appropriate quality, PMI will continue to support strengthening of the National Drug Authority. [Funds for this activity are included under the Pharmaceutical Management section.]

- **Monitor drug resistance (efficacy) of antimalarial drugs:** Drug efficacy studies are conducted every two years. As FY 2013 PMI funds will support the next cycle due in 2014, this activity will not be funded again until FY 2015.

MONITORING AND EVALUATION

Background

According to the Uganda National Malaria Prevention and Control Monitoring and Evaluation Plan 2007-2012, the goal of the national monitoring and evaluation system for malaria control is to provide reliable information on progress in controlling malaria. The specific objectives of a national monitoring and evaluation system for malaria control in Uganda are as follows:
- To collect, process, analyze and manage malaria data
- To verify whether activities have been implemented as planned to ensure accountability and address problems that have emerged in a timely manner
- To provide feedback to data providers and relevant authorities to improve future planning
- To document periodically whether planned strategies have achieved expected outcomes and impacts

Improvements have been made in Uganda in the monitoring, evaluation and surveillance of malaria over the past several years. Measureable achievements include: (1) finalization of national M&E plan for the years 2011-2015; (2) revision of the HMIS with increased malaria representation and a more cohesive and coordinated support for the national roll out; (3) completion of the 2009 MIS and the 2011 DHS; (4) development of the NMCP's first performance monitoring plan; and (5) development and publication of a quarterly malaria bulletin. However, challenges remain within the NMCP's M&E unit including a non-functional database, inconsistent data receipt from partners, and lack of dissemination of data to stakeholders for programming use.

PMI Uganda has used the following tools to measure the impact of malaria control efforts:

- **The 2010 Anemia and Parasitemia Survey:** Provided information on anemia and parasitemia in children under five years of age and district-level ITN coverage data in two districts with and without IRS in Northern Uganda, with similar distribution of ITNs and support for case management.

- **The 2011 ITN Coverage Survey:** Provided information on ITN and other malaria intervention coverage at district levels in the central region of Uganda after the targeted mass ITN distribution campaign in early 2010.

- **The 2011 Uganda DHS:** Provided data comparable to the 2006 DHS as well as anemia levels in children under five years of age.

- **The 2012 Uganda RBM Impact Evaluation:** Will provide an analysis of malaria activities for the past ten years and their impact on key malaria indicators and all-cause under-five mortality.

- **Evaluation of parasite prevalence of 2004 and 2011 AIDS Indicator Survey samples:** Will provide baseline and mid-term parasite prevalence information for PMI activities using Polymerase chain reaction (PCR) technology. A reprogramming request has been submitted to use FY 2012 funds to conduct this work. The protocol is under review by CDC country support team before it is submitted to the full OR committee.

- **The 2014 Uganda Malaria Indicator Survey:** Will provide national and regional-level coverage and impact data on the four major malaria interventions as well as biomarkers for anemia and parasite prevalence in children under five years of age and will be used as an evaluation of the effectiveness of the Global Fund Round 7 Phase 2 ITN distribution campaign and a mid-term point for PMI activities.

Progress during the last 12 months

Surveillance activities
The malaria sentinel surveillance sites continue to provide high-quality longitudinal data from 12 health facilities - six outpatients and six inpatients – located in different malaria transmission zones across Uganda. The NMCP and partners as well as PMI use the data to understand the burden of malaria in the catchment areas served by these facilities. Cases reported from the surveillance system are laboratory confirmed and can be considered to be valid and reliable, and can be used to assess how malaria has changed over time in these areas. The data are used at multiple levels of the health system and by malaria partners for planning and tracking progress of interventions towards malaria control. Through workshops dedicated to dissemination of findings, the program has positively impacted case management practices by clinicians at health center IVs and hospitals. A robust quality control system for microscopists has been initiated and the results indicate excellent performance in terms of slide reading accuracy across all sites. In December 2011, an assessment of the surveillance system was conducted and concluded that the data are of high quality and the system is supported and managed well by the implementing partner.

2011 Demographic Health Survey

The 2011 DHS report was finalized and the report disseminated. The report shows gains in coverage of key malaria intervention strategies such as ITN use up - to 60% from 16% during the previous DHS IN 2006. ACT use among febrile children also increased from 1.1% to 30%.

Strengthening HMIS and NMCP data management

When the HMIS was updated in 2010, USG support to the system was also reorganized to ensure that a comprehensive and uniform support is provided for the entire country. The USG implementing partners provide support for printing tools, follow-up support supervision, training, data transmission (weekly surveillance and routine monthly data), and data dissemination to the Ministry of Health Resource Center (responsible for HMIS) and for select districts. PMI continues to support basic equipment at the district level to improve data collection and reporting (e.g. internet connection and internet technology maintenance); and has introduced data quality assessments in select districts.

Following the roll-out of mTRAC, the MOH's mobile phone based tool to collect surveillance and malaria stock data at the health facility level, USAID implementing partners such as Stop Malaria and NU-HITES have begun to support District Health Teams to improve reporting rates, and to action the data being reported, especially around reported stockouts of ACTs. The emphasis in the coming year will be to support Districts with providing refresher training to health facility's on using mTRAC, and facilitating transport for redistributing ACTs between health facility's , with a particular focus on PNFP HF's which appear to be disproportionately stocked-out relative to public health facility's.

PMI continues to support the M&E unit of the NMCP; the focus in FY 2012 was the revision of the national M&E plan, the performance monitoring plan, partner mapping and reporting, and the malaria database. The malaria database, which is based on the WHO GMP template, is designed to contain intervention program data (number of nets distributed, number of houses sprayed, etc.) as well as epidemiologic data (malaria morbidity, mortality and other malaria indicators). The database, if fully functional, could provide NMCP with the ability to readily store and retrieve key malaria data in harmony with HMIS. However, several activities must be completed in order for the NMCP to fully utilize the database: (1) update the database with current data; (2) train the NMCP M&E staff in the use and maintenance of the database; and (3) develop the operating procedure for the database. Given the critical need of quality data by the NMCP, PMI will continue to assist the NMCP to develop and maintain a functional database.

Implementing partner monitoring and evaluation

PMI contributes to support a USAID/Uganda Mission-wide data collection mechanism for all implementing partners. This project assists partners develop performance management plans, collect data and conduct data quality assessments.

Data Source Table

Data Source	Year[5]							
	2009	2010	2011	2012	2013	2014	2015	2016
Household surveys[1]	UNHS 2009/10

UNPS 2009/10

UMIS 2009 | UNPS 2010/11 | UNPS 2011/12

UDHS 2011

UAIS 2011 | UNPS 2012/13

Child mortality survey | UNPS 2013/14 | UNPS 2014/15

MIS | UNPS 2015/16 | UDHS

UNPS 2016/17 |
| Other Surveys[2] | | | | | | | | |
| Malaria surveillance and routine system support[3] | Sentinel sites data

HMIS | Sentinel sites data

HMIS | Sentinel sites data

HMIS | Sentinel sites data

HMIS | Sentinel sites data

HMIS | Sentinel sites data

HMIS | HMIS | HMIS |
| Other Data Sources[4] | | | | | | | | |

Proposed PMI activities with FY 2014 funding: ($2,775,000)

- **Support malaria reference centers:** PMI has supported malaria surveillance since 2006. In order to leverage the significant lessons learned from this work and based on the recommendations from the PMI external evaluation to develop a long-term approach to malaria surveillance, malaria surveillance sites will become district malaria reference centers (while continuing their role as malaria surveillance sites). These centers will provide training, technical assistance, and quality control and assurance to the surrounding health facilities on case management (focusing on the use of diagnostics and adherence to results), and the collection, analysis, and use of routine data. Any support provided to health facilities will be focused and resource efficient, based on lessons learned while establishing the initial sentinel sites. The first set facilities to be supported will be in Apac District where IRS is currently being carried out. The (proposed) district malaria reference center will enable the collection of appropriate epidemiological baseline data from supported health facilities, and monitor any change over time as IRS strategy is updated. Given the surveillance expertise developed over the past five years and the long-standing collaboration with district staff where the reference centers will be located, PMI expects the new implementing partner (TBD) for this activity to have the necessary capacity to manage this expansion. ($500,000)

- **Program monitoring and tracking system development – districts**: PMI will continue to support the HMIS at district and health facility levels, in coordination with the overall USG support from USAID, PEPFAR, and CDC. With FY 2014 funding, PMI support will focus on collecting timely malaria data using HMIS. PMI funds will also support training of the persons involved in collecting and analysis of malaria data at the district and health-facility levels. ($750,000)

- **Program monitoring and tracking system development - NMCP:** PMI will continue to support the M&E unit at the NMCP to improve their capacity for data collection, analysis, and reporting. ($100,000)

- **PMI data collection and reporting**: PMI will continue to support the USAID/Uganda Mission-wide M&E Project to serve as the central data collection point for all implementing partners. ($100,000)

- **End-use verification**: PMI will continue to conduct End-Use Verification surveys annually in 20 randomly selected health facilities in four districts to determine the extent to which antimalarials are available at the end-user level and how effective supply chain systems are used in managing malaria commodities. The End-Use Verification surveys provide useful data on supply chain management and malaria case management, which can be used to strengthen the health care system through informed decision making. ($100,000)

- **The 2014 Uganda Malaria Indicator Survey**: Will provide national and regional-level coverage and impact data on the four major malaria interventions as well as biomarkers for anemia and parasite prevalence in children under five years of age and will be used as an evaluation of the effectiveness of the Global Fund Round 7 Phase 2 ITN distribution campaign and a mid-term point for PMI activities. ($1,200,000)

- **2 TDYs from CDC-Atlanta**: CDC staff will provide technical support for M&E activities including the HMIS, 2014 MIS, malaria reference centers, and operations research projects. Two visits are planned to ensure adequate follow up of planned activities as one visit would not adequately cover all on-going activities. ($25,000)

CROSS-CUTTING BCC

Background

Since 2001, the NMCP has revised its malaria communication strategy three times to incorporate new developments such as home-based management of fever, malaria prevention during pregnancy, and the treatment of uncomplicated malaria using ACTs. The current communication strategy supports Uganda's Malaria Control Strategic Plan and its implementation is supported by guidelines and communication tool kits. The strategy, guidelines, and tool kits are designed to provide an integrated communication plan that standardizes messages and tools for all partners working on malaria in Uganda. The strategy recommends various channels of communication from one intervention to another, based on specific attributes of the target audiences, such as literacy levels, access to television or radio, and other social and economic characteristics. In general, households and families are reached using radio, community drama, printed materials, community and religious leaders, and through community support groups and household visits.

The over-arching goal of PMI's BCC program is to enhance and facilitate access to comprehensive malaria prevention, diagnostics, and case management services. The program reinforces existing innovative and effective BCC campaigns through mass media and interpersonal communication to create and increase demand for malaria prevention and treatment services in both the public and private sector.

Progress since PMI launch

PMI's efforts to date have focused on national, district, health facility, and community levels. PMI has focused on changing attitudes and modifying behaviors of targeted audiences through well managed BCC programs. The main audiences for focused PMI BCC programs have been communities at large, community leaders, pregnant women, children, caretakers, health workers, and drug dispensers. However, there is still a great need for BCC requiring a sustained effort especially at the lower levels to encourage behavior change for consistent and correct net use, early diagnosis, prompt and effective treatment. This is because PMI recognizes that healthy behaviors of families, communities, opinion leaders, and providers are critical to achieving PMI goals.

Challenges

Although there has been progress in terms of key malaria indicators in Uganda, some critical challenges remain. The 2011 DHS showed that only 63% of children under five years slept under ITNs the night before the survey in the households with a net, showing the need to further reduce the gap between availability and use of ITN s. Despite more than 90% attendance at antenatal clinics in Uganda, only 25% of pregnant women completed two doses of SP during their last pregnancy in the DHS Survey.

The NMCP targets for BCC vary depending on the intervention, the funding available, and the behavioral problem at hand. However, the M&E component to assess how the BCC targets are met has been weak and only a few specific BCC indicators have been developed. Most activity reports generated for BCC activities cover process indicators such as the number of people reached and carry limited information on the impact of the BCC activities on the malaria profile in the Uganda. A baseline study is planned through the new soon-to-be-awarded Uganda Mission BCC mechanism; lessons will be drawn from this study to inform strengthening of the BCC M&E.

Opportunities

The NMCP has BCC focal persons at the national and district levels, and a senior health educationist to coordinate advocacy and social mobilization activities at the national level. This position supports all malaria interventions. At the district level the district health educator is designated to coordinate BCC programs in liaison with the Malaria Focal Person (MFP).

Uganda has a BCC technical working group (TWG) that was established in 2008 to coordinate activities across partners. The TWG meets whenever need arises, with the primary function of developing and reviewing communication strategies. The TWG is also responsible for reviewing the technical content of all BCC messages pertaining to malaria to ensure accuracy and harmonization of messages.

Progress in the last 12 months

PMI supports BCC as a cross-cutting activity focusing on all interventions: case management including diagnostics, ITNs, and IPTp. The current IRS contract also incorporates a BCC component. In the last twelve months, PMI activities continued to focus on: 1) key behaviours that need to be emphasized, i.e. regular use of bed nets; and prompt diagnosis and treatment with ACTs for patients with fever; and 2) the main incentives and barriers (and how to overcome them) to practicing these behaviours, through the use of various BCC channels such as radio and TV shows and adverts, community drama, and village meetings. In the last 12 months PMI activities reached 4 million Ugandans with key messages around net use, care seeking, and IPTp through radio talk shows, 247,794 school children, 244 community listening groups, and through village health assistants' community mobilization and school activities.
With core and field support FY 2012 funds, PMI is supporting two studies in Uganda. The first study is intended to provide information on social behavior regarding net washing, how households/communities value nets, magnitudes of misuse of nets as well as types of net misuse. The second study is addressing the aspect of care and repair of LLINs after the universal coverage distribution in four Eastern districts that was carried out in August 2012. It will be a prospective study to "watch" what happens to a net from the point of distribution to the point of wear and tear. A strong BCC program will be part of one arm of this study to document differences in household behaviors in regard to care and repair for nets. The results from these two studies will be available in late 2013 and will be used to improve BCC activities funded through PMI.

Plans and justification

PMI will continue using the tracking tool that was developed in 2011 by the BCC Working Group to assess the impact of previous BCC efforts with FY 2013 funds to provide guidance on how to prioritize FY 2014 activities, including actions necessary to improve poor IPTp2 uptake. The assessment will also provide useful background information for the plans to address the importance of diagnosis as well adherence to test results. In addition, the baseline study planned through the new Uganda Mission BCC mechanism will include questions to assess impact of BCC efforts, and the feedback obtained will be used in improving current BCC efforts in all intervention areas. Effective approaches will be identified and adopted for continuation in FY 2014. Based on this assessment, PMI will continue to provide support for all types of BCC at national, district, and community level.

Proposed PMI activities with FY 2014 funding: ($900,000)

- **Increase awareness, demand, uptake and usage of malaria prevention and control interventions:** PMI will support targeted and evidence-based BCC at national, district and community level to encourage consistent and proper use of ITNs, usage of IPTp by pregnant women, prompt care seeking for suspected malaria and parasitological-based diagnosis and appropriate treatment for those with confirmed malaria. A major focus will be placed specifically upon creating demand for diagnostics and appropriate treatment as well as adherence to prescribed treatment by health care providers. BCC will be done through radio messaging and health communication at the facility level and within the community. ($900,000)

HEALTH SYSTEMS STRENGTHENING/CAPACITY BUILDING

Background

Uganda struggles to provide high-quality services in all parts of the country, especially the hard-to-reach and rural areas. While USAID programs support technical assistance to improve human resources for health in the country, the systemic challenges in recruitment, retention, and effective and efficient human resource management remain at all service delivery levels. For example, while all facilities offer malaria treatment services, only 50% of health facilities have functional and reliable laboratory diagnostic capacity.

Building NMCP and MOH capacity to implement effective malaria control activities continue to be PMI's priority in Uganda and is an integral part of PMI's contribution to strengthening the national health system. Wherever practical, PMI has implemented malaria control activities together with other major health programs, particularly those for maternal and child health, routine immunization, HIV/AIDS, tuberculosis, and other vector-borne diseases. PMI focuses on the following areas:

- Strengthening health information systems
- Building leadership and technical capacity in national malaria control programs (NMCPs)
- Linking and integrating malaria and maternal and child health services
- Supporting pharmaceutical and supply chain management
- Improving laboratory diagnostic services

The private sector continues to play an important role in the delivery of health services in Uganda, with more than half of the population seeking care from the private sector as their first point of entry into the health system. More importantly, the PNFPs provide affordable services in many rural and hard to reach areas, though the quality of service is variable.

Progress in the last 12 months

Recognizing these gaps, PMI, USAID/Uganda, PEPFAR, and the GOU have increased the emphasis on heath system strengthening. PMI plans to continue providing direct support to heath system strengthening via its own programs and integrated support with USAID/Uganda and external partners. In collaboration with PEPFAR and other USAID health programs, PMI supports improving workforce policy and planning through strengthening human resource information systems; supporting development and implementation of evidence-based human resources strategies; strengthening human resource units within MOH, local government and NMCP; advocating for policies that increase workforce retention and productivity; and developing in-service and pre-service training plans aligned to the actual needs.

With support from PMI, HRH strengthening efforts have resulted in an increase in the wage bill, and recruitment of additional staff in key cadres, especially at the HC-4 level. Consequently the number of staff positions filled has improved to ~70 %.

PMI support to the private sector has led to increased private sector involvement in malaria control through the creation of a pool of six private distributors of LLINs, a robust social marketing platform for malaria products including nets and ACTs, and the engagement of at least 15 major corporations that invest their own funds to provide malaria services to both their workers and surrounding communities. With PMI funds, NMCP received support to print the NMCP's Strategic Plan and M & E Plan 2011-2014; and the recruitment of two fellows under the Field Epidemiology and Laboratory Training Program (FELTP). The two fellows will be trained in epidemiology and disease outbreak investigation.

Capacity-building of the NMCP is continuously supported by the two PMI Senior Technical Advisors and two Malaria Program Management Specialists on all aspects of malaria control activities and programming. These advisors have played key roles in the country's malaria technical working groups. Since 2008, PMI has also equipped the NMCP with its day-to-day operations, including support for computers and accessories, scanners and photocopiers. PMI also supports four quarterly RBM/NMCP partner review meetings each year and participates in the technical working groups for all intervention areas. PMI through USAID's human resources for health program has initiated the implementation of comprehensive support to strengthen the functions of the NMCP.

Proposed PMI activities with FY 2014 funding: ($680,000)

- **Capacity building support to NMCP:** PMI will continue to support the NMCP to strengthen coordination with malaria stakeholders through RBM coordination meetings, and supportive supervision for district-level program implementation. PMI will also continue targeted support to NMCP to improve its ability to carry-out its managerial and operational responsibilities. ($100,000)

- **Field Epidemiology and Laboratory Training Program (FELTP):** PMI will support strengthening of national capacity for program planning, management and monitoring through practical field placements of recent graduates in well-performing malaria programs where they can be mentored by experienced program managers (both GOU and non-governmental organizations). Through these placements, the graduates will receive on-the-job training. This initiative will fund at least two students to follow the malaria track in CDC's two-year Field Epidemiology and Laboratory Training Program (FELTP) in partnership with Makerere University School of Public Health. ($150,000)

- **Human resources for health:** PMI will continue supporting the USAID/Uganda sector-wide initiative to address human resource shortages and develop the capacity of the health workforce at national and district level. This support will help prioritize the recruitment, retention, and performance of health workers who will address health issues with the greatest burden on Ugandans, including malaria. USAID/Uganda's district-based programs will implement the HRH support package (including leadership capacity development, performance management) developed by the USAID/Uganda HRH technical assistance program. PMI's investment leverages over $2 million of PEPFAR and other USG health investments for this area of health system strengthening. This activity will also include support for central /national MOH leadership training. ($300,000)

- **Peace Corps / PMI collaboration** PMI will support placement, training, and small scale malaria projects through third-year Peace Corps Volunteers, and their counterparts to prevent, control, and treat malaria at community level. ($30,000)

- **Support to pre-service training:** PMI will support updating the curriculum for malaria case management in key institutions that train clinical staff. This will include each cadre of health workers potentially addressing malaria (doctors, clinical officers, different levels of nurses, midwives). Once the curriculum is developed, it will be rolled out to the schools across Uganda. ($100,000)

STAFFING AND ADMINISTRATION

PMI staff in Uganda is comprised of two Malaria Technical Advisors (one CDC and one USAID), who provide oversight to all PMI-related activities in Uganda, and one USAID Program Management Specialist who supports the management and administration of PMI activities. The PMI Uganda team is planning to add two additional dedicated Program Management Specialists to the PMI team to further support the management and administration functions of the program.

The PMI team is situated within the USAID/Uganda Service Delivery Team and the infectious disease sub team. The service delivery and infectious disease team leaders are involved in strategic planning, budgeting, cross-cutting issues, and linkages with broader Development Objective 3 (DO3) and Mission efforts. The health team is part of DO3, which coordinates health, HIV, and education efforts to improve the health and education status of Ugandans.

All PMI staff members are part of a single interagency team led by the USAID/Uganda Mission Director, with-day-to day leadership delegated to the health office director. The PMI team shares responsibility for development and implementation of PMI strategies and work plans, coordination with national authorities, management of collaborating agencies and supervision of day-to-day activities. Candidates for these positions (initial hires or replacements) are evaluated and interviewed jointly by USAID and CDC. Both agencies are involved in hiring decisions, with the final decision made by the individual agency.

The PMI team oversees all technical and administrative aspects of PMI, including project design, managing malaria prevention and treatment activities, M&E of outcomes and impact, and reporting of results. All technical activities are undertaken in close coordination with the MOH/NMCP and other national and international partners, including WHO, UNICEF, the Global Fund, DFID, private stakeholders, and district officials. PMI also collaborates closely with other Mission colleagues on cross-cutting issues and ensures that PMI activities are well-coordinated with USAID Mission goals for sustainable development in Uganda; and to ensure a cohesive approach to the GHI principles. Staff members from CDC and USAID headquarters provide additional technical support to the Uganda-based PMI team and, when needed, provide on-site technical assistance.

Proposed PMI activities with FY 2014 funding: ($1,935,000)

- **Management of PMI**: Support two PMI Malaria Technical Advisors (one USAID and one CDC) based at the USAID Mission in Kampala, including all work-related expenses (e.g., travel, supplies), and three dedicated Ugandan staff, and program administrative and support costs. ($1,935,000)